THE TRUTH SHALL MAKE YOU FREE

"Freedom", they cry "freedom"..., the nations surge, people rage, as the need for a…. 'Truth'…. that will bring everything to Peace, must be found, for the 'True' system to reign.

DAVID HARNARAYAN

WESTBOW®
PRESS
A DIVISION OF THOMAS NELSON
& ZONDERVAN

WestBow Press books may be ordered through booksellers or by contacting:

WestBow Press
A Division of Thomas Nelson & Zondervan
1663 Liberty Drive
Bloomington, IN 47403
www.westbowpress.com
1 (866) 928-1240

ISBN: 978-1-4908-6284-2 (sc)

Library of Congress Control Number: 2014921858

Print information available on the last page.

WestBow Press rev. date: 04/02/2015

CONTENTS

DEDICATION

To,

    My parents, Hollick and Esther, their great love,

    provision, support,… care.

    Sas and Pat, their wisdom and strength.

    Candy, listening, understanding, together in one.

    Shan Jaénai, beauty and inspiration.

    JESUS CHRIST…… 'LIFE', IN…. 'HIS KINGDOM'….

"Why do the Nations … rage…, and the People plot in vain things? The Kings of the Earth set… 'themselves'…and the Rulers take counsel together,… against… 'THE LORD'…, and… against… 'HIS ANOINTED'…"

Psalms 2:1, 2 Acts 4:25

They seek the… "Ways"… of "Self"… and so… 'Man'… is not even aware of how… 'he'… rebels against… 'THE FATHER… OF CREATION',… 'THE LORD OF HOST'…, 'IN CHRIST JESUS'…

"'HE'… has 'DELIVERED'…us from… 'The Powers of darkness'"… and conveyed us… 'INTO… THE KINGDOM'… of… 'THE SON OF HIS LOVE'… 'IN'…whom, we have,… 'REDEMPTION'… through… 'HIS BLOOD'…, the… 'FORGIVENESS'… of sins…

Colossians 1:13, 14

INTRODUCTION

The "knowing of who you are, what and where you should be in life, permits the opportunity to achieve true 'freedom' and the ability to experience the complete soundness of soul. It is only when a noted change occurs, can then a confirmation be made that you were in bondage, captivity and now 'freed' having the "experience" to assist others in achieving 'freedom'. So who is indeed 'freed' and how does one "know", about 'freedom'?

We "know" that the World operates from established Laws, Rules, Statutes, and Standards, which are originally derived from 'THE LAWS OF GOD,' from Religion at the centre of Cultures. One thing is certain, that regardless if one fears 'GOD'… or not, reverences or not, the 'POWER OF GOD'… will always be unstoppable in their lives, as a witness for all to notice. It is the 'PRESENCE OF GOD'…, "CREATOR"… of Heaven and Earth, that is so amazing, awesome, marvellous, wonderful, shaking everything back into place and order, as example to all. This is the only reassurance in Life, as a "source", for those unavoidable afflictions, crises, fear, destruction, that we encounter. We have an assurance that only 'GOD'… can "Deliver" from such, through personal relations, which is the heart of Religion.

Only the 'One True God' can present Himself, above all others, through the ability to be "Creator", but do something more outstanding and it is notably significant that, going beyond the formality of all

"Gods", that "one", steps forward being very personal, in offering 'Relations' with "Man" It is remarkable that this 'GOD' presents 'Himself' as 'THE FATHER'..., and personalises the adaptation of 'HIS Laws'... for us not to fail, but succeed in pursuit of "relations"! The highlight of this system is found in the failure of Mankind to abide with "GOD", who Communed with 'HIS'... "People," through 'HIS Laws'... for us not to fail, but succeed in pursuit of "relations"! Due to the failure of 'Mankind' to abide with 'GOD', who communed with HIS People and BLESSED them with a 'Man Of God' sent from 'HEAVEN', 'THE SON OF GOD', 'IN HIM'.... was made available, the 'Deliverance' and 'Forgiveness' of sins and 'SALVATION' from the evil in this World. This 'Man', changed the thinking and ways of the entire World, which all Nations agreed 'IN'... 'HIS'... act of 'Self Sacrifice' to "die" for this "cause" "purpose" and as such, all dates of our historic existence are converged to ... 'HIM'! The reality of the 'Truth' is that 2000 years ago, all recorded dates, revert back to 'HIS' ... remarkable establishment referred to as B.C., "Before Christ", and all following that cenotaph of time, until today, as after A.D. "THE YEAR OF THE LORD"...!

What was so important about 'JESUS THE CHRIST' ...., that contains a 'TRUTH'..., so hard to accept, not in what 'HE' ... accomplished, but in how it causes us to change from "self-ways" to seek 'HIS WAY'....? 'SON OF GOD.... SON OF MAN'..., KING, LORD, MESSIAH, SAVIOUR, is now presented as 'GOD THE SON,'... completing the "works" of 'GOD THE FATHER,'... and is now our 'HIGH PRIEST,'.... over all works, of man and "the enemy". No more is "HE"... Judged and "Crucified" by men, no longer overcome by hanging on a "Cross", but in the "Manifestation" of 'GOD'...., as 'HE' ... said "I AM, THE WAY, THE TRUTH, and THE LIFE, no one comes to 'THE HOLY FATHER', except through 'ME'...." JOHN 14:6.

This is the 'TRUTH' that Nations seek, 'HE'... is 'THE TRUTH OF GOD',... and in John 8:32

He declares that you shall 'know' THE TRUTH, and THE TRUTH... shall make you free. HE ... 'THE KING'.... 'JESUS CHRIST'...., lived in equality with all "Men" teaching the 'Unity of the Faith' and how to avoid the "self" value, that divides, competes, cheats, confuses, causing strife, poverty and sin, which weakens society.

The most significant and amazing, awesome, magnificent 'TRUTH', that causes mystery and controversy is, 'IN'... the "RESURRECTION" ..., overcoming all the works of the "enemy" death being the worst! Therefore 'IN HIM'.... is 'THE LIFE'..., John 14:6; 1:3, 4, 9, 10; 11:25. This 'MIRACLE'... the 'POWER OF GOD'..., has caused nations to roar, and the 'TRUTH'... to be discredited. If those who had 'HIM'... "CRUCIFIED"..., 'knew' the 'TRUTH'..., they would have their system of operation overturned by 'JESUS THE CHRIST'... "Raised" the dead, hundreds of various 'MIRACLES'..., that all could not be recorded. History records Governor Pontius Pilate, asked 'HIM'... if 'HE'... was a King and discovered beyond that fact, that 'HE'... came" to bear Witness of 'THE TRUTH'...." John 18:37. "It is for this cause, purpose 'I' came" in John 12:27 "to this 'Hour'"!

The main question most try to avoid, even those in "High" places, is 'HE', 'THE HOLY ONE OF GOD' .... 'THE CHRIST', 'GOD THE SON'...? and therefore are you are ready to "obey" all that 'HE'... requires, directs, commands?

Amazing, awesome, magnificent is 'The POWER of the PRESENCE'..., the "Manifested" ... 'PRESENCE Of GOD'..., Do you "know" 'JESUS THE CHRIST', have you had an "experience" with 'HIIM'…, to "know" the 'person' character, that causes all who encounter, to never be the same again, the "passion", burning inside, to need that "abiding presence" Become just like 'HIM',… and desire to share this revolutionary 'TRUTH'… with everyone, for it is priceless!

They raised their voices to 'The Lord" GOD'…, with one accord and said 'LORD, YOU' are 'GOD', who made 'HEAVEN' and Earth and the sea and all that is 'in' then; by the mouth of your servant said

"Why do the Nations rage and the people plot vane things? The Kings of the Earth took their stand and the Rulers were gathered together, against 'THE LORD'… and 'HIS CHRIST'…"

Now oh, 'LORD',… look on their threats, and grant to 'YOUR'… Servants, that with all boldness, they may speak 'YOUR WORD'…,

By stretching forth 'YOUR HAND' … to "HEAL"…. and that signs and wonders may be done through the 'NAME'…, of 'YOUR HOLY SERVANT'…. 'JESUS THE CHRIST'…"

And when they 'PRAYED'…, the place where they were assembled together was "shaken" and they were all "filled" with 'THE HOLY SPIRIT OF GOD'.., and spoke the 'WORD OF GOD'…with boldness….

Acts 4:24-31.

BREATHE

As one seeks to go past the shrouded veil of the built up, "man" made environs, to the basics that existed before technology, to the fabric of the forefathers, there are no limits to an unfolding Kingdom, which has endured through time.

If one can "experience" the layers of unfolding simplicity, there is an existing array of limitless expression in a beginning, with its path. This is the place of 'TRUTH'...!

Whether, it is at the soft trickle of the stream, in the quiet, shaded, slopes, where the crayfish or agouti, are not afraid to move in your presence. The little pools flow into each other, form a connection; the branches of overhead timber towers embrace their branches, regardless of type, shape or colour. Vines tighten the embrace, for the bird that chooses to rest, and weave a nest.

Maybe, it will be at the flow of the stream that slithers past the rock where the heron talks to the rock crab that the vast ocean still rolls at the "voice" of the Creator. It is here, voices of "man's world" will no longer dominate. And you may hear that still, soft 'VOICE'...., that will speak to your soul; your heart will flutter with joy, as a babe does, with mom or dad. Listen, and you will "know" 'THE TRUTH'..., and the 'TRUTH'..., shall make you "freed"! Go sit, let your shoe less feet, feel the tingle if the lapping waters, allow your lungs to take in the feel of purity, feel the ground between your toes, touch a rock, that was pushed up by the 'HAND OF LIFE'… ages ago, and hope, that you will receive that touch in the midst of your soul's awakening …'GOD, SOVERIGN, ALMIGHTY',… Come, enter in, you "know" 'THE WAY, THE TRUTH' and 'THE LIFE"… that makes you "Complete."

BLESS YOU

'JESUS'... told them to go tell the things that they saw and heard; ... the blind see and the lame walk, the lepers are cleansed and the deaf hear;... the dead are ... 'Raised'... up and the poor hear... 'THE GOSPEL'... preached to them; and "...'BLESED'... is anyone who is not offended because of ...'ME'..."

Reference Matthew 11:46

1

THE GREAT PROVISION

The "awakening" of each new day, brings the reality of possibilities, relative to one's life, also the awareness of what can be expected. As the permutations and combinations of choices arise, the appropriate 'knowledge' is vital, prime, for deciding in the flow, amidst the flood of "Life's" matrix. In dealing with others, we need to depend upon our skills and abilities for proper relations and seek the best results.

Information provides the mental, meta-physical requirements to operate, and though our worlds are greatly controlled by technology, computer programs, they were "written" by 'Man' so, our interaction with superior powers beyond our world, of '...THE CREATOR'... is critical for operations.

It only takes one valuable piece of "information" to challenge one's entire life establishment, experiences and cumulated, structured status, even one's identity. Our "beliefs" therefore depend on what 'TRUTH'... we use for, determining our progression and existence.

'Truth' acts as a source when establishing and securing our works and desires, the best source, would therefore be "The Creator"...! The amount of establishment we can then experience seems relative to our stability in Life's progression. Truth then is our comfort, confidence....!

The 'BIBLE'.... declares, that you "shall" one way or another, sooner or later, 'know' 'THE TRUTH',... and that 'THE TRUTH'..., "shall" make you free! John 8:32. A very powerful word "shall," certain and sure, there is 'Promise' in its representation.

Noteworthy, is the dependence of "freedom" upon 'THE TRUTH'..., therefore our security in life is relative to 'TRUTH', all Laws and Governance, depend on the established "TRUTH"...! One reality here is the statement of John 8:32, being a message from 'GOD'..., and a call to possibly seek 'HIS TRUTH'... So, sound the "alarm", here is 'GOD, SOVERIGN ALMIGHTY'.... declaring our "freedom" to be based upon ... 'TRUTH'..., and most certainly according to 'HIS STANDARDS'.... We also note, that when 'GOD'... 'THE CREATOR, POSESSOR'... of 'HEAVEN'..., and Earth and everything within these, say "shall", then that issue must occur. Whenever "HE'... declares you "shall" receive, according to 'HIM'... then it must come to pass, unless you are not prepared!

'THE MAN OF GOD'..., 'JESUS THE CHRIST'.... referred to as 'SON OF GOD'... 'SON OF MAN' also made profound statement "I AM... 'THE WAY, THE TRUTH' and 'THE LIFE'..., no one comes to 'THE HOLY FATHER, GOD'..., except through 'ME'...! John 14:6

'JESUS, CHRIST'... declares that 'HE'... is 'THE TRUTH'..., and we also heard 'HIM'... state, that you "will" 'know' 'THE TRUTH', and 'THE TRUTH'... "shall" make you freed! John 8:32. Well, this certainly provides for our comfort and security, having the offer for "knowledge" of established 'TRUTH'..., the 'TRUTH OF GOD'....

'JESUS CHRIST'... provided for our comfort and confidence, with an 'Invitation', that continued a very profound 'Promise', of powerful enrichment to our "being", in the Word John 15:7. "If you "abide" 'IN ME'... and 'MY WORD'... "abides" in you, you will "ask", and it 'shall be done' for you, as you desire"! Wow, what an expression of open invitation, from 'GOD'… 'SOVERIGN, ALMIGHTY', and at the same time 'GOD, HOLY FATHER, ABBA'…, to enter into "relationship" Enter into 'The Abiding', 'In His Word', His World, Kingdom' an extremely grand, mighty, awesome, "opening" at personal relations, and intimate with 'FATHER, GOD'…. Note the use of "Shall."

It is also important to remember, the 'Invitation' from 'THE Prayer' given to us by 'CHRIST JESUS'… "THE LORD'S PRAYER… for us",

"YOUR KINGDOM, OH 'GOD'…, come be established, on EARTH, just as 'IT'… 'KINGDOM',… is established 'IN HEAVEN'…, so that, 'YOUR WILL'… for us BE done, accomplished, in our lives, here on earth, just as 'IT'… is done 'IN HEAVEN'…" We should pay attention to 'THE KINGDOM OF GOD, IN JESUS CHRIST' that has "come" and "if" we 'abide' 'IN HIM'…, 'HIS WORD'… we will, we "shall" be able to 'abide' 'IN HIS KINGDOM'… And "if" we 'abide' note the pivotal "condition" of the "if" that if we 'abide', we will be able to "ask" and it 'shall be done' for us! One of the most profound and "Powerful" declarations, our "FATHER GOD,'…. through, with, 'IN CHRIST JESUS'…, that the least we can do, is be respectful, relevant and pay attention to all that is associated. We have a "major" opportunity to not 'receive' only the requests of our desires, but, to 'Enter In' to 'Living Relations'! Wow. Pause, ponder, do not loose focus on 'THE PROMISE'!

Let us do some more "revealing" and establishing of 'GOD'S TRUTH'… In the statement, of promise and purpose, "You "shall" 'know' 'THE TRUTH'… and 'THE TRUTH'…. "shall" make you free", John 8:32, look also at 8:31, the pivotal conditional 'if', and 'The Abiding' "if you 'abide' "In MY Word", then and only then, you will be able to 'know' 'THE TRUTH'…, and only then will you be able to become 'freed'! This is 'TRUE FREEDOM'…. 'FREEDOM… IN

CHRIST, JESUS'...! Pause, take time to let it soak in, register, you should read this over again, do not assume it is received and fully benefited. 'THE WORD OF GOD'.... is "ALIVE"..., 'IT'... was with 'GOD'.., so powerful in manifestation, potent to "create" life, 'IT'... was 'GOD'.., 'THIS WORD' also became 'Flesh' 'IN JESUS THE CHRIST'... and dwelt, abided, among us ! John 1:14.

We must, guard, protect, that which is entrusted and provided, because the masses of the World, do not 'know' and can not accept responsibility, when the 'enemy' of 'GOD', and 'THE KINGDOM OF GOD'... was given power by "Man" to rule over the majority of this World, see Luke 4:6. Generations, have innocently, unknowingly, opened "doors" that gave opportunity to the corruption, contamination, deceit and evil, even 'death'!

The root of all conflict, disorder, atrocities and damaging ways, comes from the 'enemy', but we must not let this system of operation, keep our eyes on the source of evil, but seek to stay 'IN THE ABIDING PRESENCE OF GOD'....! 'HE'... has offered, and poured out of 'HIS HEART'..., through "LOVE", for all of mankind, humanity, to come, enter in, to 'LIVING RELATIONSHIP'..., come, to 'THE LOVE' this World does not 'know' Mountains will move, piles, heaps of hurt, mistrust, frustration, suffering, seek, knock, ask, and "it shall be done" for you.

John 15:1, 2, 4, 5, 6, 7, 8, and 9 teach and explain what and how the establishing will work, for our gain and benefit. Consider yourself, person, as a 'branch' of 'THE TREE OF LIFE'..., abide and do not become withered, through deceit, or innocent ignorance, do not be removed, taken away, from 'THE ABIDING PRESENCE OF GOD,... IN CHRIST JESUS'...., do not end up in the "fires" of life that can destroy. "Abide" 'IN HIS LOVE'..., "know" 'HIM'...!

"For without ...'ME'..., you can do nothing." John 15:5

'THE KINGDOM OF GOD'... has come, is established, here on Earth, just as 'IT'... is 'IN HEAVEN'...., so that as we 'Abide' 'IN THE KINGDOM'... here on Earth, 'HIS WILL'... for us, will be accomplished, be done, just as 'IT'... is done 'IN HEAVEN'...!

'If', the conditional "if", we choose to seek 'first' 'THE KINGDOM OF GOD'..., in all our decisions, pursuits, goals, and seek it 'IN THE ABIDING'...., then all that we need, "shall be added" unto our lives. Matthew 6:32, 33. 'THE WORD OF GOD'... states, to also seek 'HIS' "RIGHTEOUSNESS"...., and operate 'IN'... it; thus you may become responsible, trustworthy. Our 'own' righteousness will lead us into misguided deceit, and even become 'self-righteous", not aware of the 'justification' that develops could bring greater areas of issue and complications, with negative results.

'GOD, IN CHRIST JESUS'..., working 'in Him' has presented, the desire to have 'Alive' 'Living Relations' with us. John 14:21, 23, explains that by keeping... 'His Word' directives, instructions requirements, commands, that in this lifestyle 'He' "invites us to" and stay 'IN', we would be 'Loved' and... 'He' will "Manifest" 'Himself' to us. 'He' and 'THE FATHER GOD..., will make their 'HOME'..., in 'THE ABIDING'...., with us, we will have unbroken 'COMMUNION.' When, 'JESUS'... says 'I WILL'... it must come to pass...! "The Promises."

'JESUS' 'THE CHRIST'... "reveals" 'THE HEART OF GOD, THE FATHER',... John 17:21-23,

That 'IN HIM' we become 'ONE'... with 'FATHER GOD'..., 'PERFECT IN ONE'...! The desire for worldly potential, which is natural to us, puts up strong contrast, and put us at, but we are to become "CITIZENS" of "THE KINGDOM" on Earth just as it is "IN HEAVEN'... Remember 'HIS'... statement, an open declaration to come

'I AM'... 'THE WAY, THE TRUTH, THE LIFE'... John 14:6. "IN HIM... is The Life" reference, John1:3, 4, 9. There is more to discover, but we will get to it a little further on, other Chapters, but "know" this "Because 'I' 'Live', you will 'Live' also" John 14:19.

The conditions of a soul, is of prime concern, paramount; we seek to accomplish, achieve, for the provisions, protection, establishing of our needs, "But God" 'He' is intent that we 'Know' ourselves, as was designed, "specific", that we discover our gifting, abilities, and specified 'Purpose" The great "Miracle" to "GOD, IN CHRIST"... is the "Reconciling," "Restoring", "Re-establishing" through 'Rebirth" of the "spirit" and "soul". Not renovating, patching, adjusting but a "New Life" as was intended, 'Purposed', from the womb! Colossians 3:10; 2:10.

My own life was well balanced, "in" 'CHURCH'.... not just on Sunday morning but, assisting in all areas, willing to encourage, offer 'Prayer', according to 'THE WORD'..., constantly writing, studying "recording". Yet, could not believe, not understand, how I ended up on the extreme perimeter of 'THE KINGDOM'... living from day to day, no idea of a "future", just another "soul"... a nothing, nobody. Finally, I come to the place of hardship, joined with those in "the struggle", and lived in the forest area, learning a lifestyle of survival, hope of a future. 'Faith' turned to "Hope", and though all things are possible, I had no "Communion", the "ABIDING PRESENCE," seemed beyond my ability to access. Hope sat in a place that could only be a form of encouragement, "But God"! 'JESUS'... "promised" to be with us always, Matthew 28:20, but the "Footprints Story" could not put wind in my sails, but when I accepted my "mental, spiritual" death, then I was able to become stable, secure "trustworthy" to manage, maintain 'The New Life', it came to me and I would not let go! If indeed you have heard 'HIM'... and have been taught by 'HIM'..., as 'THE TRUTH'... is

'IN JESUS'…, that you put off, concerning your former conduct, the "old person" which grows corrupt, according to deceitful things and ways and be renewed "in the spirit" of your 'mind,' that you put on the "New Person" which is created according to 'GOD'…, in 'TRUE' Righteousness and 'HOLINESS.' Reference, Ephesians 4:21-24. You have become a 'New Person,' renewed in 'Knowledge' according to 'The Image' of 'HIM'… who created. Reference Colossians 3:10.

We try to 'salvage' "restore" obtain the materials of progress, but, letting go is in the opposite to gathering, gaining, progressing. Human nature seeks to survive, prosper, establish, but we must become "emptied", and must show 'trust,' which is the core, 'FAITH'…. The 'Revelation' for me was to emerge from the "World" of "Religion" to the place 'IN RELATIONSHIP'! 'IN HIM'… 'IN HIS KINGDOM'… has on earth, just as 'IT'… 'KINGDOM'…, is 'IN HEAVEN'… so, when someone becomes emptied of "self" concept, and the "old" ways, thinking habit, actions, reactions, "die", and behold, all things, are made 'NEW'! 2 Corinthians 5:17. Everything must go, no justifying of any part, characteristic, quality, ability "Trust" …'In Him' who made you, to 'COMPLETE'… what the enemy messed up at childhood, every human being, all! You are "COMPLETE… IN HIM". Colossians 2:10. The surgeon must have the wound cleaned first, completely, no remains, even of blood, tissue. Baby bottle cleaned, wiped and aired.

This is what 'BAPTISM'…, is all about, and 'JESUS, CHRIST'…., allowed John 'THE BAPTIST'… to publicly complete, the example that we must be 'Born Again' of the "Spirit," "Soul", and the "Water", representing, death, burial, and then 'The Resurrection' "Newness of Life." John 3:3, 5, 7. 'JESUS'… 'THE CHRIST'… gave the 'True', in reality, example of "Death" and removal of "self," the old person, to become 'Perfected', and complete, fulfil "Purpose". 'He' was the example, able to 'Return' to 'COMMUNION'.., with GOD, THE HOLY FATHER'…, and "sit", at 'HIS RIGHT HAND'...! We must, follow 'His' "example", and remove the old self and receive the 'New Person', soul and spirit. 'He' did not "Die" only to provide for us, the 'FORGIVENESS' of "sins", because we continue in it, expecting continual "Forgiving". 'He' "Died", and was ...'RESURRECTED'... to overcome all the "works" of the enemy, 'death' being the worst, that we too can be "Spiritually Resurrected", overcome and even destroy the working of the enemy. John 'THE BAPTIST'... established 'BAPTISM'... transformation, through "repentance" 'JESUS'... established complete "soul condition" to 'ABIDE... IN THE KINGDOM,'... and 'ETERNAL LIFE'...!

We can 'Repent', and receive 'Forgiveness', but the 'complete' works, requires the 'Transformation' to an intended, purposed, "soul" that the enemy will flee from, because of 'THE ABIDING PRESENCE OF GOD THE SON'...., the enemy cannot affect the human mind and soul, ...'ABIDING, ... IN HIM'...

"'He' will 'BAPTIZE'... you with 'The Holy Spirit' and 'FIRE'"! As specified, John 1:12, 13, those, who are 'Reborn', not of the will of blood, nor flesh and blood, not the will of 'Man' but 'THE WILL OF GOD'...!

When anyone, has an "EXPERIENCE"...., with 'JESUS THE CHRIST'..., that one will never be the same again; it is only through experience, can one finally "know" something or someone. It is only by spending time with one, that you can 'know' that one. 'HE'... overcame all the possible works of the enemy so 'Enter In', to 'THE RESURRECTION LIFE'.... 'In Him' was, and is 'THE LIFE...', JESUS'... the same, yesterday, today 'now', and forever. Hebrews 13:8. 'He' is 'PERFECT'.... "know" 'Him", today, Hebrews 1:2, 3 a 'New'... and Living, Alive'... "Way, Truth, Life"! Hebrews 10:20.

'He' gave us 'THE RIGHT'..., 'THE AUTHORITY'... to become 'Sons, Daughters of 'GOD'... 'IN CHRIST'... John 1:12. So those who "know" 'HIM,' go "therefore", because they "know THE TRUTH"..., and fulfil their 'Purpose'! The Directives, Instructions, Requirements,' Commands', were not for those in 'MINISTY'... then, and certainly not now, but all for all are 'CALLED'... to 'CHRIST JESUS'... to become 'CHRISTIAN'..., according to 'CHRIST'..., and from 'CHRIST'... The 'Inheritance' for the ' Sons, Daughters' awaits you, all 'Authority', ' IN HEAVEN'... and on Earth, given "to 'ME', go therefore" This is 'THE FREEDOM'.., nations cry out for it, no one can 'DELIVER'... but only 'THE ONE'..., 'THE CHRIST, JESUS. Matthew 28:18.

The book of Isaiah Chapter 53 describes 'HIS SUFFERING'..., for us, "fulfilling" the 'PROPHECY' of more than two thousand years. 'THE OLD TESTAMENT' ... a 'GOD'..., establishes 'HIS POWER'... and works in and among 'Man', but, 'JESUS THE CHRIST'... is 'THE NEW TESTAMENT OF GOD'... 'POWER, TRUTH of GOD,'... world, without end. The Book of 'THE NEW TESTAMENT" teaches us how to exist, live, operate, after 'His' physical departure, but 'ALIVE'... with, 'IN HIM'..., 'HIS KINGDOM', here on earth, just as 'IT'... 'KINGDOM'... is 'IN HEAVEN,' so that as we "Abide", 'HIS WILL'... 'THE WILL OF THE HOLY FATHER'..., is done, in our lives, on earth, just as 'IT'... is done, accomplished 'IN HEAVEN'...

Do you "know" 'HIM'...? You shall 'know' 'THE TRUTH'... and 'IN'... 'HIS PRESENCE' which is 'THE TRUTH'..., you shall "make yourself free", will not require 'HIM'.... to do anything. Your NEW person, will desire to "Abide" because 'HE'... made you, 'GOD'... through 'CHRIST JESUS'... John 1:3, 4, 9, 10, Ephesians 3:9, Colossians 1:16, Hebrews 1:2, 3. 'JESUS'...is the 'THE TRUTH'..., 'HE'...is 'The Freedom'! John 14:6; 8:32

Note the word "shall", the certainty, surety is as the working of Law, 'THE LAWS of GOD'...! It must come to pass.

Note that 'THE DESCIPLES'..., were prototypes of 'CHRISTIANS'... for the 'CHRISTIANITY'... of 'JESUS'... Upon maturing, all the works and results can be accomplished by anyone. All are 'CALLED'... Ephesians 4:1, 4. Note Romans 8:28 and reference to "Purpose"!

"And we 'know'... that all things work together for good to those who love 'GOD'..., to those who are called, according to 'HIS PURPOSE'..." That the intent being, for the "Purpose" of each soul to be 'fulfilled'..., during their life time.

2

THE REASON

The accomplishing, of the "trustworthy" 'New Soul' is only achieved, when the 'Witness' is received from THE LORD, JESUS CHRIST'..., approved, accepted, to then be confirmed amongst 'souls', here on Earth. Only when one has the "experience", will one 'know', otherwise like many, basking in emotional and intellectual condition, not coming to 'THE KNOWLEDGE OF THE TRUTH'... This is the "place", a 'spiritual, metaphysical condition of first, needing to live "IN THE ABIDING PRESENCE"... it is 'Perfect'. Second, desiring to become just like, 'CHRIST JESUS',.... to not just 'experience', but become, love, peace, goodness, kindness, caring, patient, considerate, wise. Thirdly, you will not be able to keep away from sharing this 'PERFECT TRUTH'...., everyone must 'know', and become 'BLESSED'..., as you have received this treasure. You will 'know' that your "being" is in this world, but contained all together in a much greater, magnificent, world. John 8:32

When we were young, pre teen into that time of adolescence, and the family visited from abroad, foreigners, we tried to soak up all the goodness of that advanced culture, but also, try to become, just like that character. We want to be as educated as their culture provides, to nurture, cultivate the nice, thoughtful, considerate, kind, grace, giving nature. After they depart, to their land, for weeks we still try to culture 'ourselves' but most of it gets lost, in the thick of our own culture and "world". Well, an encounter with, 'JESUS CHRIST'.., should affect us in the same way and as we seek more of 'HIM'... through 'HIS PRESENCE', we will want to become just like 'HIS'... 'PERSON'. John 14:6. We seek "The Way' "The Life" and "know" of 'THE TRUTH', this is "freedom" of soul, mind, lifestyle, that cannot be left, unless in a place of mental stress, torment, depression. The first "CHRIST-IANS".... were the 'ones' that followed 'HIM'... not physically, but mentally, spiritually and therefore called... 'THE CHRIST like Ones', 'Those of the Way'. "PURITY"… transcends their World, and the "witness" of it, touches souls, transform minds, ways, thinking, habits, attitudes, it is so amazing when 'HIS PRESENCE'... "appears" and the effect on those who do not "know" it. They become amazed at an unknown "catalyst", seeing, experiencing 'change,' in and around everyone, everything, as a witness, 'testimony', a reality of new dimension.

Freedom is always preceded by an established 'Truth', but the working of 'GOD'S TRUTHS"... of 'HIS KINGDOM'..., always brings change, and many cannot accept change. The enemy, who is the author of confusion, tries to dissuade, disappoint, and create disaster "but GOD"..., only 'THE CREATOR'... can establish "order". Faith is based on the decision to ' Trust' and stand firm not waver, or give up, but human emotion, can cause many to be disillusioned and hold on to imaginary "truths", believing to have 'faith' that will move "mountains". Faith, is different to hope, for we seek the assurity of what, will happen, not hoping that something will happen. 'Faith' is the substance, evidence of what is expected to occur, that one is willing to invest in that result. Hope anticipates, something can, may or will happen, and if 'GOD IN CHRIST'.., makes a result occur, then to shout "I knew, 'He' could do it," but not be certain if 'HE'... would, will do it..! Many come to 'Prayer' lines for Ministering, but not sure if 'HE'... will do anything for them, or if it is their time, 'HE'... can but will 'He' perform?

The 'WORD OF GOD'... declares, that the 'faith' of those ' IN THE KINGDOM OF GOD'..., is like that of a man, who discovers a "Treasure" in a field, and not knowing the size or value of it, goes out and sells all that he possesses, to purchase that particular plot of land. Understand, it sounds easy, but he did not use his "savings", he sold all his, possessions. Will one be able to sell house, car? That is a whole different situation. It is shocking, that when facing adversity, and affliction, to not have the 'LORD'... change the situation, provide 'DELIVERANCE'... many are devastated to 'know' they had no 'Faith' and in fact, no real "relations" as was believed. GOD does not 'DELIVER'..., because of pity, 'He' feels sorry for us, nor is it because of our righteousness, and good deeds. Change must occur when we become 'Trustworthy' to not re-enter the cycles of problems, or become repeatedly snared with other tricks of the enemy. 'THE LORD' cannot keep ...'DELIVERING'... and we keep getting "DECEIVED" repeatedly, we must be ...'Transformed'... to become stable, reliable, ...'Trustworthy'... to manage, maintain, the 'New Life.'

'THE LORD GOD, HOLY FATHER' through, 'IN CHRIST JESUS', does not want to keep fixing and adjusting, as some parts affect others, 'HE' wants to "impart" a New Life. In Ephesians' 4:21-24, it is 'THE TRUTH' that causes us to receive the changes within the soul, our conduct, which was corrupted at childhood, by atrocities and wickedness of the world, "to cheat, steal, beat, kill,"! We need to become renewed the 'spirit souls', and put on the "NEW PERSON", created according to 'GOD IN CHRIST'.... in 'TRUE'... righteousness, as 'HIS RIGHTEOUSNESS' exist, and the 'Purity' of 'Holiness'. Do not be scared, 'Holiness'... is the "Purity" of truth, righteousness, honesty love, kindness, caring, mercy, it does not dictate the life of a Priest for you to adopt. Ephesians 4:13-16, explain that we will grow "in" all things 'INTO'... 'CHRIST"'.., to the fullness of "HIS"... stature to a "perfected" person. That, the ways of the world, of "Man" will no longer knock us around. We become as a "body", 'THE BODY OF CHRIST".... this is the term used to collectively identify... the members of 'THE CHURCH',... the CHRISTIANS, that come together, a 'SPIRITUAL BODY'... not a building full of people. We each will fulfil our own 'Purpose' and then come together, operating as a 'Body'..., all 'IN CHRIST'.

Human nature does not see the minor attributes that are common, and overlooked, we do not see the "negatives": "judge, non-forgiveness, angry, covet, lust, greed, irresponsible, mislead, discourage, self-pride." When one is suffering, it is impossible to be taught that "change" must occur, for ' THE DELIVERANCE'..., but the mind of the soul, is focused on relief from pain, suffering. One is not able to attain to teaching, in this condition, this is the example, again, for you to attain, that, 'JESUS THE CHRIST'..., did not only 'DIE' for our 'Forgiveness' of sins, but, to provide a 'NEW LIVING WAY', to be 'Transformed' as 'He' did, to be, 'Perfected' fulfil 'Purpose.' 'IN HIM'... we will be able to overcome and destroy the works of the enemy, not just for us, but everyone, because 'He' overcome even "death"!

We love the 'SCRIPTURE', that says "we 'know' that all things work together, for good to those who love 'GOD'..., to those who are 'CALLED' according to 'HIS PURPOSE'..." Romans 8:28. Having been 'CALLED', those who answer, respond, to the 'WILL OF GOD', they cannot operate through their own evaluation, understanding, but 'HIS'... "STANDARDS." All are 'CALLED'... Ephesians 4:1,4 to be "discipled", trained, taught," "CHRISTIANITY" according to "CHRIST"..., not religion. "CHRISTIAN"... to, of from 'CHRIST'.....

Remember, the teaching "if", you abide "IN HIS WORD"...the "TRUTH" will then be accessible to you, and only then will you be 'Freed'! John 8:31, 32.

The great misconception that causes a majority of misfortune, deceit, affliction, comes from the concept, that everything which was "instructed, required, commended," in 'THE GOSPELS' and 'THE NEW TESTAMENT',... applies to those only, who are in 'Ministry' or 'Service', The directives were for every 'believer', all 'CHRISTIANS'..., but that which 'Jesus' directed, to the 'DESCIPLES' is label as being for 'MINISTRY', and not applied to the general 'CHRISTIAN BODY". We can seek the simple, comfortable "Christian Life", but will be as "babes" and yet we have to make adult decisions, so it won't work. 'Knowing' one's own "person" and the life that applies, are the requirements for discovering one's 'Purpose', and the gifts, abilities, to fulfil it. Without our personal 'purpose' it will be unrecognizable when one is going astray from that "path"; too far, too late, is usually when the discovery is made. We all, at one time also conducted 'ourselves' according to the "ruler" of the world, until 'CHRIST'... appeared, Ephesians 2:2,3, as if blinded by the "GOD" of the world, veiled from.. 'THE TRUTH'... and many perish. 2 Corinthians 2:2-4. The great entrapment by the enemy is in our nature to need and desire much in life. The enemy studies us, closely all our characteristics, and personal weakness, that we can be lead away from 'THE WAY, THE TRUTH, and 'THE LIFE'...! 'THE BIBLE'... refers to us as "lambs to the slaughters' like sheep among the wolves. The 'matrix' of all the choices available, is designed by the enemy to provide that which will appeal to our needs and desire, specifically; we become conditioned to increase our "desire" and provided with products, lifestyles! Trouble! Do we pay attention to each detail of our lives, daily? Well the enemy does, to learn to 'know' and then plan!

Now let us look at... 'THE LIFE'... we are forced to 'Live' enslaved, in bondage! The "TRUTH'... becomes cloudy, unrecognisable; we become confused, then imprisoned. Listen, think, let your heart, not mind, but your 'heart' listen with 'JESUS THE CHRIST'

REVELATION 1

In the 'beginning'......

Perfect environment conditions, for every need, provision, in a system that was "planned" and by its 'CREATOR' specific in details. The intended "lifestyle" was determined, to be centred "in" the 'CREATOR's' personal relations, 'THE PRESENCE OF GOD THE FATHER'... This arrangement ensured that the "first children" will be shaped, developed, from direct 'Living Relations' and every generation will follow in the same manner, for an, eternity.

The first two human, strayed from 'THE ABIDING'... of 'THE PRESENCE OF GOD'... and became 'deceived' by the enemy; they became confused with "values" and ignored 'THE WAY, THE TRUTH' and 'THE LIFE'...! The word "disobey", was not important to them because "discipline", did not have punishment, until then, the value had not yet appeared, no occurrence for it to be established. Then it was made 'known' and the consequence of "punishment", so 'Mankind' learned a new "value" in the system, a very high priced "issue". The punishment was in the form of "removal" from 'THE ABIDING PRESENCE'...., and they, Adam, Eve, were no longer allowed to "live", "abide", in the place that was "designed" for the habitation of relations, 'THE GARDEN OF EDEN'...! The 'ABIDING PRESENCE RELATIONS'.... were to be perfected in, and represented by 'THE EDEN'S GARDEN'. The "relations" were now more formal and disciplining, but 'THE LOVE OF THE HOLY FATHER, GOD'… did not change, toward them. The 'EDEN EXPERIENCE'…. was therefore the "lifeline" for the 'proposed' fate of all 'Humanity', the establishing point of destiny, for all 'Mankind' according to 'THE WILL OF GOD'!

Attention…!
Listen……. Think……. Listen…….

Inside of 'THE EDEN EXPERIENCE'…., exist the "lifestyle" of specified planning, for a destined civilization, to flow generation through generation, for an eternity throughout the Earth.

Listen……. Look……. "In the spirit"…….
'Revelation'

The next generation, siblings of Adam, Eve, were conceived "outside of THE EDEN GARDEN"…, they grew up not 'knowing' the 'EXPERIENCE'… of 'THE GARDEN'! Not Cain, Abel nor Seth or Enoch, "no one," not any one "knew" 'THE EDEN EXPERIENCE"… so, all of "mankind", followed a patterned "lifestyle" that was formed, shaped, without the example and.. 'EXPERICNCE'… of 'THE ABIDING PRESENCE'! Yes, 'Holy father God' had "relations" with them, but not as was the 'RELATIONSHIP'…, that was possible in 'THE GARDEN OF EDEN'…..

So, if "no one", "nobody" had the 'experience' for "humanity" to "live" according to the intended, purposed, specified 'plan' for 'Man', we cannot therefore work to establish a 'Lifestyle' and standards, that no one "knows" existed, no one 'experienced'! So the enemy has an easy job, messing up, trapping, deceiving, contaminating, corrupting, and stopping us, no matter how much we try, and "cry out" for staying connected to 'HOLY FATHER GOD'!

Look..... !

The type of "Personal, Intimate Relations"... that existed 'IN, THE EDEN EXPERIENCE' Genesis 2:19, having made all animals, 'THE FATHER'..., sat with Adam, as he was encourage to give them "names", sharing an 'experience' 'THE FATHER' would come at a special time, in the cool of the day, to seek Adam and Eve, Genesis 3:8. This situation changed for "disciplinary" reasoning to be established. How can we establish what never was exposed to us, each generation, after generation

But..... 'GOD'.......
Infinite 'LOVE, MERCY, GRACE,'.... through,
'IN CHRIST JESUS'...,

Came to set things back into "Order", re-establish 'Living Relations' by offering 'Reconciliation' 'Re-establishment' so come, let us... 'Enter In'! "'I AM'... 'THEY WAY, THE TRUTH..., THE LIFE'...., no one 'comes' to 'THE HOLY FATHER'... except through 'ME'..." and you 'shall' get to "know" 'THE TRUTH'... and therefore, 'THE TRUTH'... 'shall' then be able to set you 'Free'! "FREEDOM IN CHRIST"... So, "if", you "Abide", live, stay, dwell... 'IN THE ABIDING PRESENCE'..., through 'THE WORD OF GOD'..., you will be learned, taught, trained, as a disciplined one, then, access to be granted, for "knowing" 'THE TRUTH'... and obtaining "FREEDOM IN CHRIST"... You "shall know", from, 'THE LIVING WORD'... which is for us... and "manifested" into "life" 'IN JESUS THE CHRIST'!

"'THE WORD'... become flesh and dwelt among us." John 1:1, 2; 1:14.

Each person was formed "special", brought into the world, with love, care, grace, no one, none, came "in" by accident. One by one, each, with a 'purposed' life. The gifting, abilities, talents, are "known" by the 'CREATOR' so get to 'know' 'HIM'...

'The kingdom of God' is our "provision" that it come, be established, on earth, just as 'It' 'KINGDOM'... is established, 'IN HEAVEN'... so that, as we "abide" 'IN THE KINGDOM'... 'HIS WILL', be done, accomplished, in our lives, here on earth just as.... 'IT'... is done, 'IN HEAVEN'! Imagine 'THE THRONE OF GOD... PRESENCE POWER'.., millions of 'ANGELS'... 'ELDERS', here glory, glory, for us, forever! Amen.

No longer, shall we look upon 'Him', 'THE CHRIST, JESUS'... with the image of 'MAN OF GOD'... 'SON OF MAN, SON OF GOD,'.... 'PROPHET'... 'RABBAH TEACHER'... who was hung, on the 'CROSS OF CRUCIFICATION'....! No more, for... 'He'... is 'HIGH' and 'LIFTED... up, 'PERFECT'... no longer with human limits or contamination... and now... 'GOD'... as THE SON'... for us, our 'HIGH PRIEST'! 'ANOINTED, HOLY ONE OF GOD'... 'SAVIOUR'... for the world.

3

NEED FOR..... REVELATION

The 'Power' of 'God', for us, is 'IN THE PRESENCE'..., 'HIS' "Manifesting" comes with our "Abiding", which was intended, 'IN'... 'THE EDEN', no separation from "Communion". Such provides, conveys "Commune", "Community." It is "IN THE ABIDING"... we obtain 'COMPLETE SOUL', Colossians 2:10; Ephesians 1:3; 2:6. It is here we receive what is referred to as the revealing, "Revelation". This can occur any time, all the time, remember John 17:21-23 that we "all become 'ONE'.., 'PERFECT'... 'IN ONE'..."! That we all come to 'The Unity of the Faith', into one body, 'THE SPRITUAL BODY, OF CHRIST'... we grow in all things... 'INTO HIM', to become the "perfected" person, all equal 'IN HIM'... Ephesians 4:13-16.

The teaching on "THE ABIDING"... carefully explains, we are like a branch of a tree, and must therefore "Abide In", for all sustenance, existence, "purpose" "'Abide in Me' for without 'Me', you can do nothing", Then a very profound statement dependant on that pivotal "If" states that 'If', anyone "abides IN HIM",... by 'HIS WORD,' then that one will "ask", and it "shall be done" for him, her John 15:7. However, any person regardless of religion, status, that does not "abide", then that one will become withered and have to be taken away, "cast out" from the 'Abiding Presence' like Adam, Eve into the outer part of 'THE KINGDOM'..., and the 'Fires' of life will burn that one! Adam, Eve, encounter much hardship, and it became worst for each generation to follow.

It is easy to think, of one not being. 'IN THE ABIDING'..., that, it seems harsh and unfair, 'God' will not throw us into "Hell Fire" if we do not "Abide", but, it states that you will be removed from 'THE PRESENCE OF GOD'... and put into the outer parts, like an unappreciated student in class, to make way for an appreciative, attentive student. The "WORD"... teaches, that we will become withered, like a branch that is disconnected, and dries up, to be finally removed, it is here where one can fall away spiritually and become "Burnt" as in 'The Fires' of life's hardships! Reference, John 15:4, 5, 6, 7, 8 notice in line 7,8 when we have achieve success 'IN CHRIST JESUS'...., 'GOD THE FATHER'... is 'Glorified'!

It is for this 'Purpose' 'I' have 'Raised' you up, that 'MY POWER'... be seen working in you and 'MY NAME'... 'known', declared throughout the earth

Roman 9:17

Listen… Think… Soul, Heart….

A part of noteworthy 'knowledge' occurs in the way Eve, then Adam, were separately deceived by the enemy. Separation develops "self-life", self-will, thinking, actions, and the opportunity for the enemy to convince, deceive, snare! They were encouraged to develop "doubt" concerning 'THE WORDS OF THE HOLY FATHER'..., by saying "you will not surely die", from eating of the forbidden 'TREE'...! The moment their attention was gained, the distracting, "deceit" was released, telling them that they will receive information, knowledge that is for them, and also, can become just like 'THE FATHER'...! They

21

were already 'CREATED'... 'In' 'HIS IMAGE'... then through maturity will be exposed to more and more "knowledge", but the information that is above their understanding, not yet ready to deal with, was made to be seen as 'their rights', to receive. We all want as a child to grow up quickly, be like our parents, well, this 'desire' to rush in, speed up opens us to problems, and is the design of the enemy! It is now our nature, to be inquisitive, curious, to seek information that is privy to others or private for others, not our affairs. This is the problem, with being outside of 'THE ABIDING.' The design and intention, was never for us to become so persistent, constantly seeking information, knowledge. Insecurity would not have occurred, "ABIDING"... 'IN THE FATHER' Most will look at an accident or incident where someone dies, but after, regret ever looking; a child does not need to think about the details of murders, rape, pornography! So, Genesis 3:2-5, records this incident, and the punishment, is seen in Genesis 3:22-24,... 13-19. The specific type of "relationship" which God intended changed allowing adoption of freedom to question, challenge, doubt, this independence is dangerous creating "self-life" decisions, independent, from 'THE FATHER,GOD..., where all our problems begin!

The need for connecting back into 'LIVING RELATIONS'... through 'ABIDING PRESENCE' can only work, if we have "REVELATION" from 'HOLY FATHER GOD'... the "knowing" 'HIM'... occurs going beyond reading 'THE WORD'... and prayer, it comes from "experiences", which develop "relations". 'JESUS'... declared in the presence of Governor Pilate, at the prosecution proceedings, "It is for this cause, Purpose, that 'I' have come into this world, certainly gets the attention of each person who hears of the event, at least once. All have an opportunity to consider "the giving of 'HIS LIFE'..." for the sake of the 'SALAVATION'... of others. And so 'GOD'S SPIRIT'... works to 'manifest' 'CHRIST JESUS'... for us, and give us that connection, ability to 'Commune' This is why the 'BAPTISM'... from 'JESUS CHRIST'... is done by 'Power'..., working through 'THE SPIRIT OF GOD'... and creating a 'Fire' that Cleanses, Purifies, 'Transforms' This is the 'RESURRECTION POWER'... to be born again.

Truly the times of ignorance passed 'God' has overlooked, but now, 'COMMANDS' all people, everywhere, to have 'Repentive' minds, because 'CHRIST JESUS'... 'suffered' for them, and without "Change", Transformation" they will fail 'JUDGEMENT DAY'..., Acts 17:27-31. We need 'GOD IN CHRIST'... to be "Revealed", and have 'Communion', remember John 17:21-23 so, 'JESUS THE CHRIST'... is able to become 'ALIVE' to us, two thousand years unto today, because of 'THE RESURRECTION'.... that the World may "know" and receive 'HIM'... Many people use religion for their comfort and confidence, with the hoping of it to work as the process of "insurance policies" work for life, property, investment, which is all under "Law". 'JESUS, THE CHRIST'... is about 'Relationship' and personal ministering of the soul, the great Love and Mercy of this nature can never be found in the legal system, and it is for our benefit that 'GOD'... is 'Revealed through CHRIST JESUS'.... we have been 'CALLED'... to "Enter In" to 'LIVING ALIVE RELATIONS'.... through 'JESUS'...

The 'suffering' upon 'THE CROSS'.... calls us to 'RESURRECTION LIFE'..., explained in Romans 6:2-13. A provision is made, "spiritually" for you to "Enter In" to 'HIS CRUCIFICTION'..., the burial, through 'BAPTISM'...; and "Arise, through 'HIS RESURRECTION'! The message of a "Spiritual Rebirth", removing the old, for 'New' in the spirit of your mind, Ephesians 4:23, 24, come as a "sacrifice offering" to become 'Perfected' Romans 12:1, 2 explains the value.

"I beg you, by 'THE MERCIES OF GOD'..., that you present your 'self' as a living 'Sacrifice', to be acceptable to 'God', become 'HOLY', and this to be your reasonable service. Do not be confirmed to this World, but be 'Transformed', by the renewing of your mind, that you will prove, what is the good and acceptable, and "perfect" 'WILL OF GOD'...."

So, we "Enter In" to 'THE ABIDING', and receive 'PROMISE'..., for our choice! There is an account of a "certain" woman, in a "certain" village, who welcomed 'JESUS' to her home. She had a sister that came to sit at 'HIS'... "FEET", and hear 'HIS WORD'..., but this woman, Martha, was distracted, taken up, with much serving. Martha approached 'JESUS'... with a concern "LORD, do you not care, that my sister has left me to serve alone?" she was bold enough to then say "therefore, tell her to help me." We do so easily, become "self" oriented, that we actually begin to 'justify' our "selves" and our cause, or purpose. To be "self" consumed or 'self' willed, independent of 'GOD', also "invites" a "controlling spirit" into our lives. 'JESUS, CHRIST'... therefore said to Martha, that she was worried and troubled about many things, but, of her sister Mary, "one thing is needed, and Mary has 'chosen' that good part, that 'shall' not be taken from her." Luke 10:38-42.

If you also make the 'choice', to hold on, not let go, "value" 'THE ABIDING PRESENCE OF GOD'... 'IN CHRIST'..., the 'PROMISE' is for you "it shall not, be taken from you."! Believe me when 'THE LORD GOD'... says "shall", like law, it must come to pass. The decision to not "obey" 'HOLY FATHER GOD'.., in Eve, then Adam, is classified as 'rebellions' in 1 Samuel 15:22, 23 it is stated, that we should consider "rebellion" or "disobedience", as the sins of witchcraft, and "stubbornness" as the unrighteousness of idolatry. Idols distract us, control us, and eventually become "gods" for many. A controlling "spirit" is that of witchcraft. Martha was in her thoughts serving, but that works does not justify, causing the one being served to feel guilty to agree with the server's demands because of the provisions that were prepared! Remember John 14:21, 23.

'JESUS'.., personally 'PROMISED'... to be with us, always even to the end of this age or era, Matthew 28:20. In 'spirit' and in 'truth' we can expect 'HIS' "MANIFESTING". John 14:21, 23

So, John, 'THE BAPTIST' prepared a way for the coming of "PURITY"... in the extreme state, in 'THE HOLINESS OF GOD'... 'IN CHRIST JESUS'.... John performed a 'BAPTISM OF REPENTANCE'... and thousands travelled great distance to "experience" this 'BLESSING' and obtain 'FORGIVENESS', to become worthy of 'THE MESSIAH'... bringing 'THE KINGDOM OF GOD'... to them. Likewise, we also can obtain the "experience" through those things which 'GOD'... foretold, by the mouth of 'HIS PROPHETS'... that 'THE CHRIST'... would "suffer"... 'HE'... has 'fulfilled', 'Repent', and be converted, in the mind, soul, that all unrighteousness, iniquity, sins, be "blotted out" from remembrance, and that times of refreshing, form 'forgiveness' may come from 'THE PRESENCE OF THE LORD'..., and that 'HE' would send 'JESUS'..." Acts 3:18-20. What more can we ask, so straight forward and easy to understand.

There is now confidence, and comfort, in being able to "know" yourself 'IN HIM", to desire, removing the "self"... characteristic, and obtain new values, from being with 'HIM'... 'IN HIM'..., HIS KINGDOM... come, established, on earth, just as 'It. is established 'IN HEAVEN',... so that you "abide" 'IN THE KINGDOM'..., and receive 'HIS WILL'..., being done, for you, just as it is done, 'IN HEAVEN'....

When we encounter, and have an "experience" with 'THE CHRIST, JESUS',... we become filled with compassion, caring, not for ourselves, but for others, appreciating 'HIM'... and the hope for others to receive this 'TREASURE' as we have been so 'BLESSED'... It is 'Written' in 'THE WORD OF THE GOD'..., that ten lepers, encountered. 'JESUS',... and 'HE' DELIVERED... them all, then they went on their way celebrating, but one, only one, felt it important to return, and give "thanks", and he was a foreigner! The human nature is so easy to enter slackness from discipline, so by being 'IN THE WORD'... we are Discipled.

"'I' come to send 'Fire' on the earth, and how 'I' wish it were already "kindled", but 'I' have a 'BAPTISM'...., to be 'BAPTIZED'... with, and how distressed 'I AM'... until it is accomplished." Jesus, in Luke 12:49, 50

I must refer, at this point, to the time 'GOD THE FATHER'... spoke from 'HIS KINGDOM' for the third time, and those gathered, were in three categories, some that heard nothing, some that claimed it was thunder, and some that heard a "voice", but decided it must be the 'VOICE of an 'ANGEL'..! What is the point here, well, it is about 'REVELATION'.... from 'GOD' as we also today, imagine God' speaking to us. If you have a busy lifestyle, flowing in the systems of the world, and too much information being processed, as the natural human desire to 'know' receive information, obtain 'knowledge' you will not "hear" from 'GOD'...! Technology, specifically the "TV, computer screen", and the "cell phones", bombards us, constantly, all day if we choose, and as the phone wrings all the time, it becomes impossible for the brain and the mind, to connect with 'THE KINGDOM OF GOD',... the kingdom of this world, overrides us.

There was a time when I had to spend at least twenty or thirty minutes to clear my mind, slow it down, stabilize, then it would be possible to connect with, 'HOLY FATHER GOD, IN CHRIST'.... The World Systems made it difficult to connect more quickly. Instead, of asking for more 'MINISTRY'..., I sought to connect with the 'source', uninterrupted, so I asked 'HIM'... for more "time", to 'Commune', for 'THE ABIDING'... to not depart, and it was given, Remember "ABIDE"... ask, and it "shall be done" for you, and also, especially as you desire; it "shall" be.

So I asked for more "Abiding", and now my "cell phone" does not have me in bondage or enslaved. In fact, I do not want to talk on the phone much, the "experience" that I have received is of 'Perfect' fulfilment. I am "Complete" 'IN HIM'..! One will not 'know' of bondage, until 'Freed'! The movie "THE MATRIX"...., portrays the "concept" of "living a Lie", of living in a world that represent a deceitful replica of what is expected, in fantasy, not the "TRUTH". Lives need to be "Freed" into 'THE TRUTH'.... by "REVELATION". If they do not know what life should and could be, they will continue in what was offered by the World...!

The choice to 'TRUST'... in 'CHRIST JESUS'... who made the 'SACRIFICE OFFERING'... and provided an "example" for us to seek "Renewal" as 'He' obtained, is the only way to avoid the condition of the world, run by the enemy. We alone, can change the condition of the world, by trying to lead others' IN TO... THE TRUTH'... by sharing, or "witness" for others to have a "choice". Until we all come to 'the Unity of the Faith'... until the kingdom of this world, become 'THE KINGDOM'... of our... 'LORD'... and 'HIS CHRIST'... 'HE' shall reign forever, and ever. Ref. Revelation 11:15.

Another work of deceit, by the enemy, conceived in the establishing of "self-life" independent from 'GOD THE FATHER'... is the concept that we were given "Freedom of Choice"! It seems like a nice concept to teach, that one can, 'Justify' "selfish" desires. The idea is established in believing that, we were "made" by dad, mom, and when at the legal age of maturity, then one has "THE RIGHT"..., to make his, her "own"... "self" decisions! The great pleasure of experiencing the personal choices, of what one wants, when and how! This concept of "self-empowerment" seems to be the root cause of controlling attitudes, the greed, the deceit.

Actually, we were "made" by 'GOD'... through... 'IN CHRIST JESUS'..., John 1:3, 4,9,10; Ephesians 3:9; Colossians 1:16; Hebrew 1:2, 3; we are "Created" by 'HIM' for 'HIM'..., and not our 'own' desire. 1Corinthians 6:19, 20; 3:16, 17..., paid for "freedom" freed out of bondage... by 'THE BLOOD OF JESUS CHRIST'...! Note also, the point stated, 3:15.... "Saved"... through 'FIRE'..! The attempt for self control independent of 'GOD' is embedded in our cultural ways, and then religion is contaminated and corrupted. Throughout history, it is observed, that the core of culture is always centred around a supreme "power", a 'God', that affects and control everything, from nature to man. Religion becomes the system for "connecting" "relating" with the god,

Let us look at the simple power of "spiritual" revelation. When 'Jesus' had been 'RESURRECTED'... 'He' appeared to the disciples, standing in their midst, 'Revealed' to them because, they devoted their lives to 'THE ABIDING PRESENCE'....

Through 'His' "Ascending" to the spiritual realm, they will have to depend upon 'THE ABIDING", the physical will no longer be available! The coming together, as agreement, witness, of one 'TRUTH'... in 'CHRIST'... gave them empowerment to fulfil 'Purpose'. "If two of you 'agree' on Earth, concerning 'anything' that they ask, it "will" be done for them, by 'FATHER GOD'... IN... HEAVEN... For where two or three are gathered 'together' 'IN MY NAME'..., "'I AM'... 'IN,' the 'midst' of them." Matthew 18:19, 20

'Jesus asked them, "who do men say that 'I am'?" as they answered, 'HE'... then asked," who do you say 'I am'?" they were expected to look within their hearts, souls, for a "confession" of what they "Believed". Peter however, said "YOU... are 'THE CHRIST'... 'SON of THE LIVING GOD'....", 'JESUS' response in declaring that Peter was indeed, operating in, "the spirit realm", but in 'THE REVELATION'... OF... 'HOLY FATHER GOD'..., not "Revealed" by flesh and blood, but by 'THE FATHER IN HEAVEN'... 'KINGDOM REALMS'...! Peter's heart revealed that 'JESUS' was the "SON OF GOD"..., "THE LIVING

GOD" 'Alive' 'IN JESUS'..., ready for 'LIVING RELATIONS....
Reference Matthew 16:13-17.

It is because of this 'Revelation', they were ready to "know" 'HIS
PLANS'... for establishing 'THE CHRIST BODY'... and they will be
called 'CHRISTIANS!

"'I' shall build MY CHURCH'..." and proclaim also, that no other
power "shall" prevail, but 'HIS POWERS'... "shall" prevail! Matthew 16:18

The time was at hand, for establishing of 'THE MEMBERS
OF THE CHURCH BODY'..., 'THE SPIRITUAL BODY OF
CHRIST'... shocking days were to come upon them, after 'JESUS'
CRUCIFICTION',... all HIS followers would be persecuted, imprisoned,
even murdered, great fear would be released by the enemy, to destroy
"THE ESTABLISHMENT."

Look....Listen.

The absence of 'ABIDING PRESENCE' after expulsion from 'THE
EDEN', affected the offspring of Adam, Eve. Such a sad situation, in
the establishment of 'self-will' independent of 'GOD, THE FATHER'
occurred when the siblings, Cain and Abel, prepared a "sacrifice
Offering" to 'GOD THE FATHER'... in honour of 'ATONEMENT'....
'THE FORGIVING CEREMONY'... for sins. This was represented
for Adam, Eve, in the 'Sacrifice' of animals, to provide clothing to cover
their nakedness and shame, not having 'Repented' of their "sins" 'IN
THE PRESENCE OF GOD'.... For the first time flesh will then be
consumed. Cain was a tiller of the ground, and prepared an 'Offering'
from his labours, but, Abel "sacrificed" an animal, as he was a shepherd
of animals. Genesis 4:2-7

'THE LORD GOD'... respected Abel's "offering" but not that of
Cain, and he became angry, as a result, his continence fell, depressed,

but allowing anger to "enter", and later Cain killed his brother Abel...! Again, the absence of having 'THE ABIDING'... caused "self" to rule, and the first, most horrible crime and "sin" was established..., "murder"! This was a terrible Landmark of history, a most horrible event, but 'THE LORD, FATHER GOD'....spoke to him before the 'crime' "if you do well, will you not be accepted,? But, if you do not do well, 'sin' lies at the "Door" and its desire' is for you" What a statement, enough to keep him in accordance with 'The Establishment', but "self will" overcame Cain! 'THE LORD' had said to him, "sin lies in wait at 'The Door', its 'desire' is to entrap you, but, you should 'rule' over it!" The way of 'THE LORD'... is to give us enough knowledge to manage. Cain did not need any more advice; all that was needed was' THE ABIDING PRESENCE'... of 'GOD'. Man adopted that desire to 'know' all possible information, more than needed, including the dangerous parts. 'HIS PRESENCE', 'HIS WAY'... is enough.

We need the 'REVELATION'... to overcome, 'Perfect', for the flesh is weak! Because the flesh needs sleep, food, or it becomes miserable, suffers, the soul is made weak. It is very important for us to remember that the "Revealing" comes from "THE ABIDING"..! 'JESUS'... gave example, just before 'THE CROSS'... and 'HIS CRUCIFICTION'..., in Gethsemane, "FATHER... not what... 'I' will, but what 'YOU WILL'... be done."

We can have confidence to not be alone, and seek, as 'HE'... did, to 'Abide'... within 'THE WILL OF THE FATHER'... The last hours of 'HIS'... 'Freedom,' the 'Disciples'' whom 'He' asked to support 'HIM IN' Prayers, were sleepy, unable to keep up with 'HIM.' Our own "WILL"..., for survival is important to our well being, but we should seek first, 'THE KINGDOM OF GOD'... and all things, will be given into us. "THE HOLY FATHER"... 'knows' our needs before we ask. Seek 'HIM'... before making decisions from the 'choices' available, remember 'sin' awaits at the "Door" of all our moves. 'IN HIM'... 'THE CHRIST'... we shall rule over all things.., 'LORD' over us, not by "law", but 'LOVE' providing and protecting, teaching. That you will say of you 'LORD'....

"I can do all things, through 'CHRIST JESUS'... who strengthen me" Philippians 4:13

Unfortunately for many innocent "souls", they cannot, receive 'THE LOVE OF GOD'.... 'IN CHRIST JESUS'... and enter into serious conditions, situations, of severe affliction, of suffering, and can not surrender to 'HIM'... 'IN HIS LOVE'... The ability to only connect when "broken" in spirit, or emptied, stripped of all personal value, it is then, one finally "surrenders" and says "help, me LORD"..., have your way." It is truly hard, by the conditioning of this world, and the way the mind, soul, develops for one to receive "Teaching" on how to "let go" and hold on to 'THE LORD'..., for transformation of a 'New Soul', 'New Life'! As one has the experience of slowly loosing "life", hidden latent and undetected 'fears' cause the 'Soul' to hold on tight until safe. But "Trust", the element at the centre of 'Faith' will allow one to 'let go' 'IN TO'... 'THE HANDS OF THE LORD'... to 'know' that 'THE ABIDING'... is at hand, waiting on that release to 'enter' and take control. To 'know' 'HIM'... personally, makes it easy!

In foreseeing, and 'knowing' all things, especially through 'HIS'... works and arrangements for providing, 'JESUS'... declared "In this world, you will have tribulation, but be of good spirit, countenance, for 'I' have overcome the world." John 16:33. 'IN HIM'... is "THE LIFE", John 14:6.

'IN HIM'... we are not just safe, but we become conquerors, as we "ABIDE IN THE TRUTH"...., 'HE'...is 'THE TRUTH'... 'THE WAY'... and 'THE LIFE'... This is why 'HE'... also said "because 'I' live, you will live also" John 14:19. However, 'HE'... wanted us to not get too

31

carried away with emotions, be deceived, blocked from receiving, and said "the ruler of this world is coming, and has nothing 'IN'... 'ME'...." John 14:30. The message is to check your own "person", check your 'self', to be certain there is "nothing" within you your lifestyle, that can give the enemy... the ruler, cause to condemn or attacked and destroy your "life". In Romans 8:1 we learn that." There is therefore, now, no condemnation, to "those who are 'IN CHRIST'..." Those who "enter in" to 'THE ABIDING'..., those who are 'CALLED'..., and step up to, 'know' receive and fulfil 'Purpose' Romans 8:28, you can become "COMPLETE"... 'IN HIM'... Colossians 2:10, 'IN HIM'... is 'THE LIFE' John 1:3, 4,9,10 'HIS'... "OWN PEOPLE"... did not receive him, and today we want to be able, but the enemy tries to "attack" our emotions, intellect for failure. So, do not be confirmed to this world, but be 'Transformed' by the 'Renewing' of your mind, and soul, that you will be able to 'receive' and 'prove', 'THE WILL OF GOD'... Romans 12:2.

'JESUS CHRIST'... had so much more to share with the disciples, as the 'Hour' of 'HIS' "arrest" and 'CRUCIFICTION'... was close, but they were not able to deal with this John16:12 Can you bear them now? The "experience" of 'Relations" with 'JESUS THE CHRIST"... will allow us to then, be able to "know" 'HIM', and willingly choose to be with 'HIM',... "THE ABIDING PRESENCE"... and then become, just like 'HIS PERSON'...

Freedom, the nations cry out "Freedom", but not everyone will accept the 'TRUTH' of the matter; "FREEDOM ... is IN CHRIST JESUS..." not to take and go, but by 'Abiding'! Upon 'THE CROSS OF CRUCIFICTION'... 'JESUS'... looked at what will become of 'HIS' works, and the condition of the people, all nations, and said to 'THE HOLY FATHER, GOD'...

"Forgive them, because they do not 'know'" and today they still do not 'know'... 'THE TRUTH'... that will make them 'Freed'!

4

THE NEED

The 'soul' was formed from a combining of "spirit and flesh", the nature of the soul, involves being able to provide, secure, become established in life. The body does have certain requirement to stay alive, basic needs such as food, rest, recreation, cleaning The design of the body and function was changed, at the time of eating the forbidden 'Fruit' and being banished from 'THE GARDEN OF EDEN'.... An animal was sacrificed, defining the point of 'transformation,' for a life of choice, eating flesh, requiring clothing. In the end of all things, with the 'New World' and 'Life' to come, the lion and lamb will lay together, and eat straw as originally designed, so we were not intended originally to eat meat, to kill have blood flow. "Do not eat the blood", was in 'THE LAWS OF GOD'... The female anatomy changed with the monthly birth cycle bleeding, which was not of original design. Anyway, now that your minds are "open", let us look at the message to be established. The body must meet the basic requirement where the mind of the flesh will declare, "I must eat, I must sleep, must bathe, clothe, recreate!" It is in the 'Justifying' of "I must" that the "self-life" independence develops. When, hard work produce rewards, such as income, savings, homes, grocery supplies, possessions such as, T.V, bedroom, bath, clothing, it is here that the soul has 'desires'!

The requirement 'desires' make way for luxury levels, of provisions, possessions, it is here, that the the enemy will produce, provide "choices", the matrices that affect our lifestyle. We all 'know' that 'desires' produce 'pleasures', and the types of pleasure that are thrown before us, are shocking today, nudity in the news paper, on public bill boards, on the computer screen! So, overwhelming, 'desirable pleasure' becomes "justified", and we will hear "leave me alone I don't tell you who to date or sleep with, so don't tell me what to do"! It is at this point of "choices" that our secretive lifestyles develop, and much, much, excuses or 'justification'. The concept of "self-ish" focuses on the seeking the interests of 'self' but also not regarding others, and being, acting, independent from 'GOD'.

Look....... Listen.......
Think.......
Listen.......

"Whenever 'self' seeking exists, every evil thing and confusion is there!" Reference James 3:16

In James 1:14, 15; the natural desires of 'Man', male and female, seeks the matrix of options, choices, but the 'desires' that exist in us will become extended, grow, in to greater 'desires', and new 'desires' until "Passions" and "lust" develop, and these become uncontrollable. At first like all things, a few drinks, maybe a smoke, some close personal relations, whatever the pleasure, but soon all will become uncontrollable, especially the human relations and 'passions', 'lust' that become a "Fire", that needs to be extinguished if uncontrollable! The end result produces 'Sin'… which brings forth …"Death"…!

The underlying unseen problem, is in the "Desire" where 'passion, lust' give rise to producing of "appetites, cravings, hungers, addiction."!

Look....... Listen.......

"But each one, is tempted when he, she, is drawn away by his, her, "own desires" and enticed; then when 'Desire" has conceived, it gives birth to 'Sin', and when 'Sin' is fully grown, brings forth 'Death'" Do not allow your 'Selves" to be deceived.

In 'THE ABIDING'... of 'THE KINGDOM OF GOD' ..., the appetites will be healthy as according to specific design everything inside our soul, will find a place of "relation" with 'THE WILL OF GOD.' You will 'know' 'HIM' by investing time 'IN HIM'... through 'HIS WORD'... John 8:31, 32 "if" you abide, you shall 'know: THE TRUTH"...

We were made by 'HIM'... that we will choose 'HIM,' to learn, understand, "know" 'THE TRUTH'! Lets us look at 2 Timothy 3:1- 4. Here we are informed, of the era, days, where people will become lovers of them ...'selves'... not lovers of 'GOD'..., lovers of "pleasure" lacking 'self-control'. When others do not please one, then that one will seek to please "self", and develop that "self-life" "self will" acting, operating, independent from 'GOD THE FATHER'... The associated characteristics that will also be identified with this are noted in Galatians 5:20, and Romans 1:29 - 31, note that 1:32 declares these characteristics, and the lifestyle that is cultured, are "deserving of death"! Very profound and major, coming form 'the LORD, GOD'...! The loosing of "self" control and regard for other, the seeking to be independent from everyone causes "TRUST" to disappear from social relations, and the world, will begin to fall apart!

We must realize, if we put our pleasure on "hold" and we empty out our 'soul' of "self", for a while, we will not loose but gain, from the 'COMMUNION" ... with 'GOD IN CHRIST'... and the 'Revelation' of 'HIS WILL'.., for us will teach us to make 'choices' according to

'HIS WILL'... A child will fight for a toy or candy, not 'knowing' what else is available, but will throw it away for a better choice! We as the adult, will have to teach the child 'new values' to avoid tossing one bad choice, for another worse one, and to "value" the 'choice' "GOD" provides and requires.

'JESUS… THE CHRIST'... gave up 'HIM SELF',... though without sin, to provide an example for us, a way out, to removing the 'Old Person' 'soul', and become prepared, stable, reliable, "trustworthy", for 'THE NEW LIFE'...! 'HE'... become 'PERFECTED'... out of the human form, "Freed" to return to fulfil 'HIS' Purpose. So too, we are able now, to 'know' and receive this 'TRUTH'... and become 'Transformed' for the specific, intended "purposed driven" 'LIFE'...! 'IN HIM'... is 'THE LIFE'... seek for 'THE ABIDING'. Do you know, that we were 'Created' by 'GOD THE FATHER'....through 'CHRIST JESUS'... 'GOD THE SON'.... John 1:3, 4, 9. 'HE' gave life, represented by 'The Light', illumination of the spirit fire, of the 'soul' 'GOD THE FATHER', symbolically "Breathed" breath into Adam, but each one was "Ignited'... with a "SPARK OF LIFE"... from 'THE FIRE OF CHRIST'...!

It is written, in 'THE LIVING WORD'... 'HE'... will 'BAPTIZE'... you with 'FIRE', by the 'POWER OF THE HOLY SPIRIT'...! No longer is 'HE' to be in the image of a 'MAN' from 'GOD' who was 'Crucified' killed upon a cross, death had no power, 'HE'... 'is' 'THE RESSURRECTION'... and 'THE LIFE'... John 11:25 declared when 'HE'... "RESURRECTED"... Lazarus. No longer "SON OF THE MAN, SON OF GOD"..., but 'GOD, THE SECOND POWER'... of 'AUTHORITY'... 'GOD THE SON'...; and now earned the title, 'HIGH PRIEST' and 'INTERCESSOR, MEDIATOR', of 'GOD'S NEW TESTAMENT'.... and 'COVENANT'! "GRACE and PEACE" to you, from 'GOD THE FATHER'... 'IN' our... 'LORD JESUS CHRIST'...who gave 'HIS SELF'... for our sins, that... 'HE'... might

'DELIVER'... us from this present evil age, according to 'THE WILL' of our 'GOD' and 'FATHER'..., Ref. Galatians 1:4. For 'HE'... has 'DELIVERED' us by 'THE RESSURECTION'..., from The Powers of Darkness and conveyed, translated us... 'INTO... THE KINGDOM OF THE SON OF HIS LOVE'..., Ref. Colossians 1:3. Do you have this 'status' just in word or intellect, emotional imagination? It is manifested into reality and truth amidst your life. Do others bear "witness" of these experiences? This is where 'THE TRUTH'... is "known" by all those around you. Remember, the changes that occur will cause one to 'desire' the beauty, purity of 'HIS ABIDING PRESENCE'... all the time, constantly, never to be outside of it... Then the 'desire' to become just like 'HIM', goodness, peace, caring, gentle, kind, patient, considerate, wise, will overcome you. Then, you will not be able to contain, this precious "experience" and "knowledge", your condition must be to share it and a chance to convince others of this 'TRUTH'..! Bake a big batch of delicious cookies, or make bowls of delightful delicacies... and as many as want, be happy to give, and make more, giving, delivering! This is the joy 'IN THE LORD',... 'THE ABIDING IN THE KINGDOM'. It is no longer I who live, but "CHRIST"... 'IN'... me, and the 'Life' that I now live, by faith, is, 'IN CHRIST'... who 'Loved' me and gave 'HIS LIFE'... for me" Reference Colossians 2:20. The way 'JESUS'... tries to 'teach' and guide us, address the 'desires' that are common to man, we will see the value.... reflected "IN HIM"..., as the challenge keeps coming to 'The Door' to 'abide in self' and be overtaken by 'sin' Reference Genesis 4:7

The advice 'HE' gives to those having difficulty, is to 'deny' your "self" go into the soul, empty it out, and put some parts up on your own 'Cross' of responsibility, then, be 'Freed'. Follow after 'HIM', do as 'HE'... does, learn from 'HIM'... imitate the lifestyle; Matthew 16:24, 25, do not lose your life and soul! Look inside at the emptiness, and remember that "HE"... has you in 'HIS HANDS'..., be cool no one sees your emptiness and vulnerable concerns... When you become stable, reliable, dependable, "Trustworthy" 'HE'... will come to you and fill up that soul, making it "complete"; you will understand and know the 'Gifts, talents. Abilities' ready to fulfil 'Purpose', complete destiny. Colossians 3:5-10 aligns us with that destiny!

Ever consider the water buffalo, seeking to soak in the cool slushy mud waters, unlike other species, will not be stressed and traumatised if there is no waters, the pig however, loves to wallow in slush, and will fight for slush, go crazy, even produce his own with all the gunk and junk available. Regardless how long these species are kept from the slushes, if months, it does not matter, but at the opportunity to plunge in, they will always come running to it. So you, 'enter in' to 'THE ABIDING PRESENCE'... it is here for you clean, pure, "Perfect"!

Let us look again at the "Provision", for us, in Romans 6:2, 3 we are able to 'Enter In' to the 'Crucifixion Death' "spiritually", Jesus has already provided the actual real, death upon 'THE CROSS'... Then we can enter "spiritual death", thinking, habit, attitude, reactions, as the body goes into 'WATER BAPTISM'.... symbolic of burial, under the water, and then... "Arise", into 'THE PRESENCE OF GOD'...., 'IN CHRIST'..., to the 'RESURRECTION' of 'Newness of Life'! John 11:25. Do this complete procedure, with your loving 'SAVIOUR', CHRIST JESUS...! This is the 'Spiritual Baptism' that allows you to receive 'THE HOLY SPIRIT OF GOD'.... and the 'Communion' in the beauty of 'HOLINESS'; Alive, Living Relationship.

The account of what was "experienced" and the value, of 'CHRIST JESUS' .... "Offering" through 'SACRIFICE'... is explained in Philippians 2:5-8, to appreciate and benefit from the 'AUTHORITY,' that one day will cause every knee to bow, and every tongue 'confess' that 'JESUS CHRIST'... is 'LORD OF LORDS, KING OF KINGS'... 'HOLY ONE OF GOD'....

The Apostle Paul, tried to also look at the value of all that we pursue, in accomplishment, possessions, through the perspective of accounting all these things, to be as rubbish, dangerous, damaging, if 'CHRIST JESUS'... not be in the "midst" of the process. "I have counted them as a loss, that I may "gain" 'CHRIST',... and be "found" 'IN HIM'...., 'HIS KINGDOM',... that I may "know" 'HIM', and 'THE POWER OF THE RESURRECTION'. Paul was seeking to attain to the 'Resurrection', from this world that produces so much destruction and death but note, Philippians 3:7-11, that he does this by 'valuing' 'THE SUFFERING'... that "CHRIST JESUS"... endured. Does anyone want to 'know' about "JESUS"... concerns, of what was to be accomplished upon 'THE CROSS'... and what was available 'IN THE RESURRECTION'? 'JESUS' had great concern of what will become of 'CHRISTIANITY'... and the other "Gods" of man, not just religious gods, but the things that control one, money, foods, sex, clothes, cars, house, lifestyle of gods!

"That I may be found 'IN HIM'... and that I may 'know HIM'..., 'IN HIS KINGDOM'... here on Earth, just as ...'IT'... 'KINGDOM'... exist 'IN HEAVEN',... so that 'HIS WILL'... be done, accomplished 'IN'... my life as I abide 'IN HIS KINGDOM'.., this should be our "Psalm."

We are warned of "Worldliness" "Materialism", the god of this era, love not this world or the things of this world, or the 'LOVE' of "THE FATHER"... 'IN CHRIST'... will not be in you. To become dear friends, with passions, desires, for the world, create enmity, conflict with 'GOD'... 1 John 2:15-17, James 4:4.

Very direct and serious is the statement by 'JESUS'..., if anyone 'loves' father, mother, son, daughter, and I would like to add, new baby more than 'HIM' then that one is not 'worthy' of 'HIM'...! Matthew 10; 37, 38 whoever does not take up their own 'Cross' of responsibility, and follow 'after' 'HIM'... is not worthy of 'HIM'... If anyone "denies" 'HIM', that one will be "denied" before 'His Father', Matthew 10:32, 33.

Where is our 'Heart' if we truly care, and do love 'HIM', who 'LOVED' us while we still were sinners, and also 'DIED'... for us, that we might come to "know" 'HIM'... and be able to become 'JUSTIFIED'... by 'HIM'... Romans 5:8, 9. Ooh, wow, can you feel it? The book of Isaiah, Chapter 53, details all that 'HE'... "experienced" on our behalf, so it is the least we can do, to have a 'Repentive' mind, and receive times of refreshing from, 'THE PRESENCE OF THE LORD, GOD',... and that 'HE'... may send... 'JESUS'... to you 'THE ABIDING'... is where the "LIVING" is at, find 'IT'...!

'FREEDOM'... 'FREEDOM IN CHRIST JESUS'......

5

THE TRUTH REVEALED

The thought of evaluating, rationalising one's status as a... 'CHRISTIAN'..., to be secure in convincing your own soul, and everyone else, that you are going to be in.. 'HEAVEN'... after departing this world, is very reassuring, fulfilling, comforting. Our confidence lays in the establishment of 'Religious Orders', and by being connected through CHURCH relations or our family's standing, we receive a placement in the strata of recognition; many "inherit" their 'CHRIATIANITY'. Just regular attendance comforts many, but the majority are seeking something of the 'LORD'... all together, the relations needed are far from what is required according to 'HIM'..., and 'HIS' definition of 'CHRISTIAN'... should be what determines or classifies 'CHRISTIANITY', but 'HE'... looks at the heart, soul!

CHRISTIANITY, according to 'HIM'... is relative to your dealings with... 'HIM'..., personally, 'The Relationship' is what matters.

The receiving of "JESUS CHRIST"..., into one's life, is the beginning, but 'HE'... must cause that one to become not just "changed" like adding sugar to lime juice, but a complete "change", as in lime juice becoming orange juice It is here that others will recognise the pleasantry, delight, of the transformed lime to orange "juice", and then 'THE LIGHT OF GLORY' of GOD'...., will come into many lives, as "THE WITNESS". It is here, that one becomes received into 'THE KINGDOM',... 'INTO'... 'THE ABIDING'..., and declare with fullness, "I am IN HIM'. This is that 'Transforming' of soul, that cannot be understood, or attempt to be 'known' unless it is "experienced" "IN HIM"... 'THE ABIDING PRESENCE'... is where that unique "smile" emerges, that cannot come from anything or place, on this planet, except, 'THE PRESENCE OF GOD IN THE CHRIST... JESUS!

It is one thing to see the gratefulness of having received a new job, a place to live, even a personal relationship, even medically the health safe, but I tell you, when a life becomes changed, from the "encounter" with 'JESUS, THE CHRIST'... that one looks as if having just returned from a trip, holiday, to "HEAVEN"! This is it, that countenance, having been "ABIDING"... with "HOLINESS..., the "experience" that every soul actually longs to receive, that 'EDEN EXPERIENCE'... complete, Colossians 2:10. Moses after forty days on Sinai, but... 'IN THE PRESENCE'... of 'GOD THE HOLY FATHER'... returned "glowing" from 'THE GLORY OF THE PRESENCE'...!

The Revelation, of... 'CHRIST JESUS'..., will come only from the... "ABIDING EXPERIENCE"... by being in 'THE WORD' of 'GOD'... start "living" in 'THE BIBLE'... let that... 'LIVING WORD'... works as a spiritual medication, nourishment, in the soul... "Trustworthy" is the requirement to manage, maintain that which will be entrusted to you. One will become able to assist others, into the stability, into 'THE WAY... THE TRUTH... THE LIFE'... then 'THE TRUTH'... shall make them 'Freed'! The 'LIGHT'... of 'THE GLORY'... has come for all that I will say of my 'LORD'..., "MY, 'GOD'... shall supply all my needs, according to 'HIS' "RICHES"... 'IN THE GLORY'... by 'JESUS CHRIST'..." Reference Philippians 4:19

The "Book of Revelation", informs of the things that must come to pass, and also the factors already at work, now, that we should focus on the changes occurring in the 'BODY OF CHRIST'...., and the 'CHRISTIAN BODY'... in general When we see an opportunity to make our contribution that results in a difference, that a life has been "Completed," we can rejoice, relax. 'GOD'..., THE FATHER'.... desires all people to be 'SAVED' and come to 'THE KNOWLEDGE OF THE TRUTH'

'JESUS... specifically referred to 'knowing' the "signs", of change, 'IN THE KINGDOM', here on Earth. It is compared to when "Spring" season appears, everything burst into new life, system, cycles, warmth, buds, flowers, pollen, bugs, butterflies, birds, colour, fragrances. So too will be 'coming' of the 'LORD'... the quickening to the end of an era, and eventually the end to this world, and "time" The clouds will not rolls up, sun will no longer be,... but.. 'JESUS'... will be the 'LIGHT'...., Then the 'JUDGEMENT'...! The concerns for 'Heaven and Hell' are not the 'issue' but, when it is to occur, what, will we experience and the type of life to be received. Look at Revelation chapters 21:1, 22; 22:3, 4, 5 refers to the world which we will enter into, 'JESUS' is the centre of it. Revelation 22:11, 12 states that each will be dealt with according to their works, "for HIM" "with HIM"... The 'HOLY SPIRIT'... say come, invites us to drink of the 'WATERS OF LIFE'... freely..! The pouring of 'THE HOLY SPIRIT'... was given two thousand years ago, on 'THE DAY OF THE PENTECOST'.... bringing 'ALIVE'..., 'THE NEW TESTAMENT OF GOD'... 'IN CHRIST'..., and the formation of a 'NEW COVENANT' ... look at Jeremiah 31:33, 34, Hebrews 8:10-12. In the midst of the provision is offered a 'LIVING RELATIONSHIP'... with our 'GOD' according to 'HIS WILL' and 'HIS PURPOSE'... "In the midst" of offering to 'Forgive' and forget our sins, "in the midst", 'HE'... offers that we all, everyone, be able… to 'know HIM'..., and not to be taught by 'man' but by 'HIM'.. 'HIS SPIRIT' to our "spirit", 'IN HIS, KINGDOM'... here on Earth!

Note that there is a difference that has become established between 'BODY OF CHRIST'... and 'CHRISTIAN BODY'... not everyone who "sits" under a "title" is in the fulfilling of Conditions, Terms, Requirement, and 'COMMANDMENTS'...! Matthews 7:21, 23" not everyone who says 'LORD, LORD... shall enter 'THE KINGDOM'...! Many will declare that they performed mighty works, even cast out demons, heal the sick, and make many claims, but 'HE'... will say "I never 'knew' you". Many 'HE'... will not 'know'... because of "self will" and "self-works" using 'HIS BLESSING'...! But the ones who do 'THE WILL OF GOOD'..., they shall "Enter In"! Yes, this seemed tough, but in chapter 25:31-46... careful will be "separation", as with sheep and goats.... Righteous are not the requirements, not just good deeds, but those who 'know' 'THE TRUTH'... and 'abide' with it… fulfil it.

Look at Matthew 24:29, 'THE POWERS of 'HEAVEN' will be shaken, 24:32, 33, 36, 38, 39, 42, 43, it will be as in the days of Noah, eating, drinking, building, marrying, then the flood, so 'watch' for the signs and preparation required!

The 'HOLY SPIRIT'... is moving, like a flow of "liquid fuel", come drink, from the 'RIVER OF LIVING WATERS'..., Revelation 22:1. 'THE LORD', is assisting the establishment of 'CHURCHES'... new "MINISTRIES", but more anxious about... 'SALAVATION'... and the dangers of quickening "Worldliness" and 'Materialism,' that contaminates, corrupts! Religiosity is replacing 'HOLINESS'... and the 'TRUE CHRISTIAN' foothold on the earth so, 'HE' is preparing a 'BRIDE'... to become 'ONE'... 'PERFECT IN ONE'... with HIM, and 'THE FATHER'... Revelation 19:7, 9; 22:17. The title "CHRISTIAN" may not enable one to obtain LIVING RELATIONSHIP.

Let us……. Look

Listen……. Think… of…

'JESUS... THE CHRIST'....
'HOLY ONE OF GOD'....
'ANOINTED SAVIOUR'......

The image that the enemy has created, is of the 'MAN OF GOD'...., hung upon 'THE CROSS OF SUFFERING.... CRUCIFICTION'... to 'DIE' ... diminishing the 'SON OF MAN, SON OF GOD'... "Image"!

But 'GOD', 'SOVERIGN ALMIGHTY'.... 'CREATOR, POSSESSOR'..., now seen, as, 'FATHER, ABBA',... has lifted up, 'RISEN',... 'RESURRECTED'.....

'GOD, THE SON'... 'ANOINTED'... 'MESSIAH, SAVOUR'... now 'THE HIGH PRIEST of 'THE TESTAMENT'... through 'COVENANT'... and provided entry, into... 'LIVING RELATIONS'... 'IN THE KINGDOM OF GOD'... here on earth, just as 'KINGDOM' is established 'IN HEAVEN'....!

'HIS'... "HAIR",... no longer brown, as the "MAN"... of 'flesh and blood", ready to turn the soft, caring, loving "puppy eyes" into 'FLAMES'... of conviction to the wicked, the enemies of.. 'THE CROSS'..., 'HIS WORDS' not just encouraging in Psalms, Proverb, hope of Gospel goodness, but mighty, powerful, as a double edge 'Sword' cutting asunder, establishing TRUTH... HOLINESS... SALAVATION... SANCTUARY... THE WORD... is able to cut deep into the depths of the soul, and be the discerner of the intents and thoughts of 'MAN'... Hebrew 4:12.

As the apostle, John, former Disciple, relates in Revelation, Chapter 1, try to "receive" the message, be ready for 'Revelation'!

Look...

Listen…

…IN THE SPIRIT…

45

Revelation, Chapter 1, John was "in the spirit" and he 'entered in' 'THE SPIRIT OF GOD'...., then able to hear a loud 'VOICE' the sound like a trumpet, giving a 'TESTIMONY'.... He had to turn, in order to see who it was speaking. When 'JESUS'... allows us into 'HIS PRESENCE'..., when 'HE' address us, it should be at the front of us, but, regardless of status all, have to be prepared, in mind and soul, for encounter with 'HOLINESS'... Remember Moses, first time meeting 'GOD'..., take off shoes, have a feel for 'HOLINESS'..., remove "self". Moses in Exodus Chapter 3 had to leave his path, to step aside in the direction of a "burning bush", 'FIRE'! John also needed to be prepared, turning spiritually, mentally, more than physically... 'THE CHRIST, JESUS'...., was 'presented, golden banded chest, limbs like purified metal, shining in glory, strong able to endure, "white, shining countenance" powerful, light not from this world. The 'EYES'..., like flaming 'FIRE'..., more powerful, than anything that exist, like laser, together with the "POWER" of 'THE WORDS'... Sounds of echoes, like voices in accord, speaking to every language, culture, people. The 'HAIR' of 'JESUS'... was white, aglow as 'HIS'... "ROBE"... representing existence, long before the foundation of the Earth, ages and ages of existence.

'JESUS' was seen, walking amidst seven 'FLAMES OF FIRE'.., at seven 'GOLDEN LAMP STANDS'... a Power, a Purity that no man can withstand, 'THE FIRES'... being the Life, Power, 'TRUTH' of 'THE CHURCH'... The seven represent the prototypes for every 'CHRISTIAN CHURCH' to be categorised, but, behold,

'THE ONE'... who walks "in the Midst: of 'THE FIRES'..., who is called "FAITHFUL' and "TRUE"... whose 'NAME'... is 'HOLY'..., was so 'pure' so mighty, that John fell as dead at 'HIS FEET'..!

It is this identification of "TRUTH"... 'PURITY'.... 'POWER'... that cause many to surrender instantly, those of deep concern, affliction, suffering, letting of "SOUL",... into... 'HIS'...care, fall down, at 'HIS PRESENCE'..., in 'THE CHURCH'... called being 'slain' in the "spirit".

John was with 'JESUS CRIST'..., for three years, why is it neither he nor the other Disciples experienced this, also after 'HIS RESURRECTION'... 'HIS'... appearance did not cause such an effect. The mind tries to rationalize, rather than "experience"...in trust. But now, "Now, 'SALVATION'... and 'STRENGTH'... and 'THE KINGDOM'... of our... 'GOD', and ... 'THE POWER' of 'HIS CHRIST'... has come!"

But, 'He' kept John awake, though flat on the ground, to hear 'THE TESTIMONY'..., and 'HE'... did not have to lay 'HIS RIGHT HAND'... upon John, saying "do not be afraid, 'I AM'... 'THE FIRST' and 'THE LAST'... then a 'TESTIMONY'... of 'RESURRECTION'..., "I AM HE'... who 'LIVES', was dead but, behold, 'I AM'... 'ALIVE'..., forevermore"

Listen... "IN THE SPIRIT"...
...IN...

by... with, 'THE SPIRIT OF THE LIVING GOD'...

'SEVEN STARS'... in 'JESUS HANDS"... are the 'SEVEN ANGEL, SPIRITS,' of the 'SEVEN CHURCH' representations, 'THE SEVEN FIRES'...

...'JESUS'... walks, in the midst, 'HE'... is seeking those like John, who desire to come to 'HIM'.., that 'HE'... may "Lay Hands" upon them that, 'HE'... may impart 'THE RESURRECTION POWER'... unto anyone, that seeks 'THE TRUTH'... That 'HE' may empower 'THE

SPIRITUAL BODY OF CHRIST'...... 'THE CHURCH BODY' to establish THE CHRISTIAN BODY'....

> The intent, the desire,
>> That we may "gain"... 'CHRIST', and be found… 'IN HIM'...
>> That we may "know"... 'CHRIST', and...
>> ... 'THE POWER OF HIS RESURRECTION'...!
>> Look now,

That 'GOD'... 'THE FATHER'... may give to you the 'THE HOLY SPIRIT OF WISDOM'... and 'REVELATION'... 'IN'... 'THE KNOWLEDGE OF HIM'....

> That the eyes of your understanding be enlightened
> That you may 'know' what is 'HIS CALLING'...
> That you may 'know' what are 'THE RICHES OF HIS INHERITANCE'...

That you may 'know' what is the exceeding greatness of 'HIS POWER'... toward us, according to the working of 'HIS MIGHTY POWER'... which 'HE'... worked, 'IN CHRIST'... when 'HE' "raised" 'CHRIST'... from the dead and seated 'HIM'... 'IN HEAVENLY PLACES'... at 'HIS RIGHT HAND'...! Reference Ephesians 1:17-20.

> This is... 'THE RESURRECTION POWER'... for you... today... now!

Reference Ephesians 3:19, 20 "that you may 'know' 'THE LOVE OF CHRIST JESUS'... which passes 'knowledge', that you may be filled with all 'THE FULLNESS OF GOD'..., now unto 'HIM'... who is able to do exceeding abundantly, above all that we can ask or think, according to 'THE RESURRECTION POWER'... that works in us"

We are to be "imparted" 'THE RESURRECTION'... 'TRANSFORMING'... 'POWER OF GOD'... 'IN CHRIST'...,

To become 'Trustworthy' to receive 'The New Life' to 'know' your 'Purpose' note your condition, fulfil your position!

Ephesians 3:21; To 'HIM'... be 'THE GLORY'... 'IN THE CHURCH'..., by 'JESUS CHRIST'... through all generations 'HE' is 'THE HEAD' of 'THE BODY'... Ephesians 4:15; 1:22. For the afflictions of 'THE CHURCH BODY'... Colossians 1:24.

'THE QUESTION....!

So..... Listen....... Listen

"Are you ready to receive? 'THE RESURRECTION POWER'...!" check your 'self', loose 'self', look within you 'soul', is this a 'New Soul' 'NEW LIFE'...? No longer is "self" to be, but the "new person" "New Life." 'JESUS'... gave up 'HIS SELF' to become 'Perfect' again, take the example your 'Purpose' awaits!

The ruler of this world, who stands before 'THE PRESENCE OF GOD'... and accuses, looks to find something in you, to accuse, condemn, cause destruction, and send in the poison! Revelation 12:10, 11. 'JESUS'... said that there was nothing... 'IN HIM'... so check your own 'SOUL'... 'your person' look! The ruler of this World, empowered by mankind is coming! Make sure he has nothing in you to, have cause to handle and affect you! Reference John 14:30.

Enter....... In.......

Become caught up, captivated as John was on the 'LORD'S DAY'... the 'DAY' set apart for 'HIM'... Look at the "Revelation" that followed for our benefit and success. Revelation 4:1, 2 'THE VOICE'... which he had turned, to see the source, the speaker, Revelation, 1:10, 12 "spoke" again, and he 'looked' "listened", for behold, a 'DOOR'… opened 'IN HEAVEN'..., he was told, "come up here", and he... 'Entered In' to the 'THRONE PRESENCE OF GOD"....! Revelation 5:6 'IN' the midst of 'THE THRONE'..., stood 'THE LAMB'... that was "slain", now to operate, perform as 'THE CONQUERING LION'... COVERING THE TRIBE OF JUDAH'... and 'THE HOLY PRIEST, LEVITE ORDER'...!

Silence... Listen....

It is for us to "know" the 'Truth' that is for each one's, Purpose, Place, fulfil it. 'CHRISTIANS' are the 'WAY'... 'TRUTH'... 'LIFE'... 'IN CHRIST'... unto the world, that there be 'Freedom' in lands, Nations, amongst the "Peoples" 'FREEDOM IN CHRIST",.... at 'THE KNOWLEDGE OF THE TRUTH'...!

'JESUS THE CHRIST'... stood before Pilate, Governor, 'TESTIFYING' of 'THE TRUTH'... yet, he asked 'JESUS'... "What is the 'TRUTH'...?" standing right in front his sincere eyes and mind, but unable to grasp, to attain to "enter in"!

"And 'THE LORD'... whom you seek will suddenly come to 'HIS TEMPLE'..." Malachi 3:1.

Remember, we were informed that your body, is to be a 'Temple' for 'THE HOLY SPIRIT OF GOD'... to 'dwell', 1 Corinthians 6:19, 20; 3:16, 17 it says "do you 'know' this, and that you are not your "own", but belong to.. 'GOD'... who made you and secured your "Future" "Purpose" 'IN CHRIST'... by 'HIS SACRIFICE OFFERING'... 'IN HIS LIFE, HIS BLOOD'....

"Then you 'shall know'... that 'I' am in the midst", Joel 2:27, says 'THE LORD, GOD'... when 'HE'... comes for 'SALAVATION'... and for "imparting" 'THE RESURRECTION POWER'...!

So, look at the Apostle John, who sought the fresh 'PRESENCE OF THE LORD' always. At 'The last supper', he had his head on 'JESUS'... chest soaking up the affection, love, "ABIDING"..! Mary unlike Martha sat at 'HIS FEET'... to seek in all, of the 'Beauty, Purity', all 'THE ABIDING'....!

REVELATION 2

John noticed, that 'JESUS'... was very concerned, and exclaimed.. "The hour has come, that the 'SON OF MAN'... should be 'GLORIFIED'..." None 'knew' what 'HE' was referring to, then 'HE'... said "Now, 'MY SOUL'... is troubled, but what shall 'I' say 'FATHER', "SAVE"... 'ME' from this 'HOUR'..., but for this 'PURPOSE'... 'I' have come, to this 'HOUR'...!" John 12:23, 27 In 12:24, 'HE'... teaches on the concept of "Death" to be "Born again" and fulfil 'Purpose' After the falling away from 'self' and the world 'Spiritual Death" provides for 'New Life'... "IN CHRIST JESUS," reference 2 Corinthians 5:17, Ephesians 4:21-24, Colossians 3:10.

The other disciples, did not record this account, but John, the disciple who sought the fresh 'PRESENCE OF THE LORD'....; Listen... Look...!

Then a 'Voice' came from 'HEAVEN'... 'GOD'..., declaring that 'HE'... has 'GLORIFIED'... 'JESUS, CHRIST'... and will do it again. Twice 'GOD' spoke, 'THE BAPTISM OF JESUS'... and the 'TRANSFIGURATION' when 'HEAVENS MESSENGERS'.... came to discuss 'HIS' coming 'CRUCIFICTION', Luke 9:31, but this third time 'GOD'... spoke, they others did not record.

Listen....... Look in the Spirit.......

The people gathered, did not all hear... 'THE VOICE'..., some heard a thunder, and some heard a 'VOICE', claiming it must be an 'ANGEL'... Are we like these who do not hear anything, or may hear the 'VOICE OF THE LORD'... but not identify 'HIM'..., not know it is 'HE'...! But, John did hear..., and 'know'... 'THE VOICE'... and today, do we hear 'HIM'... speak...? Revelation 3:20, 'HE' stands at 'THE DOOR'... of all our opposition, adversities, afflictions, "fears", and if we "open" 'HE'... will come 'IN',... to your situation, condition and "Perfect." After this incident, John Chapter 12, they entertained.. 'THE LAST SUPPER, COMMUNION'..., and after this, 'JESUS'..., disrobed, "knelt, stooped" to wash the feet of 'DISCIPLES'... If 'I' do not wash you, you have no part with 'ME'...! We should read it as 'IN ME', not "with", so we need to be "washed" and then receive 'Transformation' through 'BAPTISM'... After this 'HE' asked, "Do you 'know' what 'I' have done to you?" The others did not record this account. JESUS then left to prepare in Gethsemane for 'HIS' arrest and end of fellowship, ministry, and life as a "man."

Note, the record of accounts, John Chapters 12,13, also 14,15,16,17, In John 14,16 'JESUS'... states 'HIS'... departure and the working of 'THE SPIRIT OF GOD'... with "man" to accomplish what 'HE'... could not do, through out the world, at one time. 'THE SPIRIT'... can "MANIFEST"... 'JESUS'..., at any time to everyone, in every nation, all at the same time..! So, 'HE'... benefited us, by leaving physically, and 'GOD'... brings 'HIM'... to everyone, all at the same moment. In John 15 'JESUS' teaches, on 'THE ABIDING PRESENCE'..., also not recorded by the others.

REVELATION 3

JOHN, Chapter17, in its entirety is a 'PRAYER'....! Look Listen! Chapter 18, begins, the first three sentences informs us, 'JESUS'... having done all these things, just crossed over a brook, Kidron, from a "Garden" which 'HE' ad 'HIS DECIPLES'... had entered

So back up, a bit, back it up, after 'THE LAST SUPPER COMMUNION'..., Judas left to arrange his business which led to the arrest of 'JESUS'... They went to "the Garden of Gethsemane", the time, of 'HIS Last Hour', to 'Commune' with 'THE FATHER'... So, they were on their way, Chapters 14, 15, 16 but 17 is 'in' 'The Garden, Gethsemane', this is 'THE GETHSEMANE PRAYER'...!. The entire Chapter 17 is this 'PRAYER'...! The accounts do not have this information, in fact there is more about the falling asleep, and not being able to support their "MASTER"... 'LORD'... Only, one sentence, stating if it be possible to avoid that final 'HOUR' of concern for what will happen to 'HIS' Disciples and followers, the 'CHURCH'... to be established, 'CHRISTIANITY.' What will become of the World! 'JESUS' was not scared of being put to suffer on 'THE CROSS OF CRUCIFICTION'... The statement, "'FATHER'... not what 'I will', but what 'YOU WILL'... be done"! One hour of 'PRAYER'...., Luke records that 'His' sweat at the forehead became like great drops of 'BLOOD'..., very intense, not fear, but concern for all "humanity", But John, seeking 'THE ABIDING'... at all times, constant "consciousness" he did not get caught in sleepiness, of course he was also tired, but 'IN THE PRESENCE'... there is 'fullness'! John caught the 'GETHSEMANE PRAYER'...!

This 'PRAYER'... of all 'HIS'... concerns, was a closure to 'HIS MINISTRY' and detailed, in Chapter 17. Much evaluation today, concerning "Religion" will cause "intellect" and "emotions" to label as a dramatic 'PRAYER'... to flow with that one comment the other

Disciples heard. But the information in the 'PRAYER' of Chapter 17 addresses the "Heart" concerns of 'GOD THE FATHER'… through 'IN GOD THE SON'… knowing 'HIS'…departure was soon. The desire for us to become 'united" together in 'ONE COMMUNION'… 'ONE SPIRITUAL UNION'… is tremendous; this should take our attention. 'CHRIST JESUS' also prayed for the World and all who will eventually "Believe" 'IN HIM'… because of the Disciples and Apostolic establishment throughout the generations, until us today! This 'COMMUNION' with 'THE HOLY FATHER'… would have given 'HIM'… closure, completeness, and that we all become 'PERFECT IN ONE'… with 'GOD THE FATHER'… 'IN CHRIST JESUS'…

If we 'ABIDE IN JESUS THE CHRIST'… we will become "complete' Colossians 2:10 and receive the daily 'revelation' that we need; our 'Communing Relationship' will perfect the "CHRISTIAN LIFE." The Disciples were an example of 'CHRISTIAN' lifestyle, not "Ministry Life," yet, John gave example of the Way, Life and 'TRUTH,' to be found, by constantly seeking, to be "complete" with 'LORD JESUS.' He moved beyond typical mind set and attitude to 'ABIDE IN THE LOVE OF CHRIST'… Later we will explore another 'REVELATION'… to establish this point, of 'CHRISTIAN TRUTH'…

'I AM'… 'THE GOOD SHEPERD'… and 'I' 'know'… 'MY SHEEP'… and 'AM'… 'known' by 'MY OWN'… John 10:14; note 10:9, 10, 11.

'MY SHEEP'… 'know' 'MY VOICE'… and 'I' 'know' them, they follow 'ME'…, and 'I' give them 'ETERNAL LIFE'…, and they shall never, "shall never" perish, nor shall anyone snatch them out of "MY HAND"…! John 10:27, 28.

Listen… Listen… to… 'THE SPIRIT OF CHRIST'…!

What is the only "Passion" worth having, that of... 'THE JOY OF THE LORD'..., the passion from awakening into beauty, love, joy, goodness, kindness, peace, tender kindness, care, concern, patience, wisdom... qualities that flood you like a "RIVER OF LIFE"...! Let anyone who 'thirst', come, drink, that it will spring up in your life a 'FOUNTAIN OF LIFE'... John 4:14... And out of your heart, soul, it shall flow like 'RIVERS'... 'OF LIVING WATERS,'... John 7:37, 38, 'HIM'... flowing.... "LIQUID FIRE"... 'FIRE'...! 'HE'... CHRIST JESUS'... will 'BAPTIZE'.... you by 'THE HOLY SPIRIT... IN FIRE!

Let us... Look..! Luke, Chapter 24:13-35. After the 'RESURRECTION'.... there was turmoil, great fear swept the land, especially in Jerusalem. 'CHRIST'... followers "Those" of 'THE WAY',... 'THE CHRIST-IANS'... were being prosecuted, beaten, imprisoned, "murdered" in this account two of the disciples, were discussing those things on the road to Emmaus,... and 'JESUS'... joined them, teaching them from... 'THE WORD OF GOD'... concerning their situation 'HE'... was not "known" to them, but 'REVEALED... HIS PERSON'... to them, and then disappeared, Immediately the 'POWER OF ABIDING PRESENCE' flooded them, over flowed their 'souls', igniting a "Passion" that 'Burned' in their heart "Did not our heart "Burn" within us, while 'HE'... talked with us on the road, while 'HE'... 'OPENED'... 'THE HOLY SCRIPTURES'... to us?" Luke 24:32

They became empowered, "ablaze" and travelled back, seven long miles after a tiresome day and journey! "FIRE"!

Does your inside begin to shuffle and shake... as something so full of 'LIFE AND TRUTH' quickens your "spirit"? Watch it; catch 'Fire', for it is 'HIS WILL'... for you!

'In HIM'... is 'THE LIFE'.... John 14:6; 1:4, 9.

"Because 'I' 'LIVE'... you shall 'Live' also." 'Shall Live'! John 14:19.

"'I AM'... 'THE RESURRECTION'... and 'THE LIFE'..." John 11:25.

Remember... Listen.... Listen.... Hear..... 'HIM'...! 'HE'... speaks to you.

6

WHERE DO YOU STAND.......?

The desire of the 'LORD, FATHER GOD'... through, with, 'IN CHRIST JESUS'..., is to provide the ability for all to come to 'THE KNOWLEDGE OF THE TRUTH'...., all to secure 'SALAVATION'... none to perish, none to suffer, become broken, emptied or stripped 2 Peter 3:9. Unfortunately, it is under these conditions that the human "soul" is able to respond and "Receive'! So we have been made 'Free', and we need to secure this 'FREEDOM IN CHRIST JESUS'...! We already discussed how difficult it is for one, in crisis and suffering, especially health issue, to be told that he, she, has to "learn" a 'New Way' The desperate search for "DELIVERANCE'..., keeps the mind occupied, hoping for encounter, but when granted may no longer seek for 'THE DELIVERER'...! So "transformation" of mind and soul is critical for becoming "New."

Both the righteous and unrighteous suffer, even, perish! We see in Luke 13:1-5, the Galileans who suffered at Pilate's hand, and mixed their blood with "sacrifice offering," or, those in Jerusalem, upon the tower of Siloam fell upon 'JESUS' asked "Do you suppose, they were greater sinners than everyone else? 'I' tell you 'NO'..., but unless you "REPENT"... you will likewise perish." Without a repentive mind, there will be peril and eventual suffering, 'JESUS'... suffered for us, so at least have a repentive mind over all your actions, and also for mercy" to fill you instead of anger, to have an "Effective"… 'Prayer'!

Do you know that before? 'THE LORD'… can answer the "Prayer" for your adversity, 'HE' has to work in you first? The preparation, first makes one acceptable, to enter… 'IN'… to 'HIS PRESENCE'…, the requirement to speak with the 'HOLY GOD'… is to also be 'HOLY'…, 1 Peter 1:14-16, Hebrews 12: 14, for without it, you will not see 'HIS PRESENCE'…, not feel, experience! So 'HE'… has to also prepare one, to avoid the "backlash" of the enemy. Then 'HE' has to let the adversary see, you 'IN HIM'…! Then, 'HE'… will go over to deal with that one, so everyone will see and witness 'HIS' working 'POWER.'

We must "bear" 'the fruit' of this 'RELATIONSHIP'… with 'HIM'… Matthews 7:16-20 declared it. Read it. "You will know them by their 'fruit'…" Many are deceived by believing in counting all their "BLESSINGS"… and trying to prove how special they are to "HIM"… and how much 'HE'… loves them, is proof of 'fruit.' Sorry, "wrong"! As we become 'CHRIST-LIKE', and produce the quality of… 'HIS CHARACTER'… then we bear 'Fruit' and others will come pick, as from a tree, and partake, then they will, like trees, bear 'Fruit.' You will not 'know' of your fruit, unless others come to "pick", so, looking in the mirror for 'Fruit' is useless!

John 15:1, 2 starts establishing the importance of possessing and proving the "Fruit", that if any one 'ANY'…, not just the Leader, Elders, Workers, Ministers, Pastors, anyone, does not bear 'Fruit', then they will be "removed" taken away! Wow. Taken out from the 'ABIDING'…, not able to cause problems, mislead others, or try to be lazy and look good 'IN THE PRESENCE'… We must bear "Fruit," be responsible for others becoming secure 'IN CHRIST.'

Notice also, that before mentioning 'Abiding' and being unable to accomplish without 'HIM'… John 15:4, 5, 6, 7, 8 the bearing of

'Fruit' is established in 15:2 Even those bearing 'FRUIT', worthy of acceptance, still have to be "Discipled' Trimmed!

Look.... Remember Romans 9:17? Go see!

Let us look at a man, who became extremely successful, Reference Luke 12:15-21. The message from 'CHRIST JESUS'... on this teaching is 12:15.

"Take heed and beware, of 'Covetousness for one's life does not consist 'in' the abundance of things that one possesses"

The focus in life, survival, establishment, is based upon "pursuit" of accomplishments, achievements, possessions. We seek to 'provide,' 'secure,' to 'establish,' and this life race has quickened, become competitive, our best values changing. The 'WORD OF GOD'... states that a certain prosperous farmer's property produced so much, that he thought "within his-self" saying, "What shall I do, since I do not have enough place to store the produce?" Then the man said to "himself", "I will pull down my barns, store facility, and build larger facilities, there I will store all my crops and goods; and I will say to my soul. Soul, you have many goods laid up for many years, take your ease, eat drink and be merry."

Please identify with this man's condition, by "speaking" to 'himself' then after, 'speaking' to 'his soul'! This occurs when one is cut off form society, or in his, her own "World"! He is also secure in his "self life" independent from everyone else, especially from 'GOD'...! The enemy encourages and causes the "self" factor. So 'GOD'... said to the man, "Fool, this night your "soul" will be required, from you; then whose will all those things be, which you have provided, for your 'self'?" Wow "Fool"! That is an Ouchy, oh that causes the "ouch"! Now he looses everything, his life, empire, all with which the farmer was so successful, but was listening to the enemy, if you are not listening to 'GOD'... to control your life, then the enemy will do it, but not let you 'know' of it. By the decision to not work, sit back and enjoy life, his discipline will be lost, a new "spirit" and "soul" will emerge. He will become a celebrity, envied by many, a terrible "role model" to the young men, stop helping employees and neighbours in their situation, quit caring for them. He will become 'self-centred,' being a man of resources, develop enemies. Now he will give less, but, expect to be highly valued, and feel very special when he does it. Many people will loose their employment stability! This is bad, but what is terrible is the "Self Life", so, the enemy who caused all this deceived him, and therefore, he lost his "Soul"! So, says the 'LORD'... "He who lays up 'treasure' for "himself" is not rich towards 'GOD' because wherever your 'treasure is, there your 'Heart' will be also" Reference Luke 12:34. "Materialism and Worldliness" becomes the Gods of many in this day, and the subtlety of "seduction" is so soothing. The gods of control, in anything that takes all our time, interest and keep us from the 'TRUE GOD'... are pleasure based, or power producing, to some it is clothing, jewellery, food, others T.V, computer, cars, or obsession with the money world, maybe sex! So "self" is where the problem originates and is creating empowered desires, lifestyles. Remember, Reference James 1:14, 15, 16. You first become enticed, tempted, seduced,... where your pleasures lies, and then the giving of more support, that 'desires' produce needs which will create the "passions" and "lusts" that produce cravings, appetites, hungers and then the uncomfortable cases of 'addiction'! There was a rebellious statement in the "70's" that if it feels good, do it! What a "Fiery" destruction with that one. The freedom of choice life style is now in full swing, pleasuring "self" and so when no one please the other, all indulge in "self life". The "Pleasures" and associated "Power" becomes the greatest fulfilment. The teaching of 2 Timothy 3:1-4 warns us of the world conditions of today and social standards, where the general interest will be in pleasing 'self', and securing relative lifestyles. "Lovers of themselves" has emerged, due to lack of care, trust and genuine feelings. Remember, the entrapment, temptation lies at 'THE DOOR' and its desire is for you! Reference Genesis 4:7. So where your "treasure" lies, there is where your 'heart' will be found!

We can choose however, to 'Abide' 'IN THE KINGDOM'... here on Earth' Just as it exist, 'IN HEAVEN', the intention is to re-establish 'THE EDEN EXPERIENCE'..., that will be in close 'COMMUNION'... with 'GOD IN CHRIST JESUS'... Without 'THE ABIDING PRESENCE'.... we are in for a long, tiresome, upsetting, "ride", many will never come back lost in "the darkness'! The most important 'factor' for us, at the core, centre of everything that exists for us, is that, 'JESUS THE CHRIST'... did not just 'Die" for our sins, but to give the example of 'transforming' the "old person, soul" into a "new person, soul" 'PERFECTED'... to complete the 'Purpose"

> So where do you 'stand'?
> Look... Listen.... Listen.....
> Think....!

Let us look at Genesis, Chapter 15. Abram, chose to stay "within" 'THE ABIDING'..., as was said before it "shall not be taken" from you, Reference Luke 10:42. Abram was a 'Transformed' man, entering 'in' to 'THE ABIDING' and never leaving, so the conversion caused 'GOD'..., now his friend, in establishing him, a 'SACRED COVENANT' was formed, and the "Sacrifice Offering" that Abraham was advised to provide, was unique. He did not question it nor be troubled, but performed; the animals were cut in "halves", placed side by side opposite to each other and vultures came down but Abram chased them away.

Later, after much wait, the sun started to go, down and he fall into deep sleep and behold, a frightening experience fell upon Abram in his lonely time This is when the hidden things of the soul surfaces and confuses, even brings doubt as one tries to purify, empty "self" for purity, for the 'Communion' that will take him to more secure fulfilling "heights" in 'LIVING RELATIONS'... with 'THE LORD GOD'... 'SOVERIGN ALMIGHTY"....

Then 'FIRE, as is the composition of a torch, together with a fire place type hearth, aflame and moving between the Sacrifice Offering pieces but did not consume it. This was a 'COMMUNION'... ceremony, between 'GOD THE FATHER'... and Abram. All other times... 'Fire' comes down and consumes the 'Offering' if it is to be accepted. In this special, personal manner, 'THE LORD', 'MINISTERED'... onto Abram, who, became a "FRIEND OF GOD"..., what a special 'BLESSING.' The 'LORD' walks through the midst of the 'Offering', having 'COMMUNION' with him.

Learn to read, study 'record' both the 'WORD OF GOD'..., and what you have learned from it. Study, the literature that come just before the place you are reading, to understand fully "what and why" of that subject area. At the beginning of the chapter, 'THE LORD'... communicated to Abram "Do not be afraid"! If however, we look at Genesis Chapter 14, we note that Abram recently had to go rescue Lot, his Nephew and his people from another raiding Kingdom. Abram was not a man of war, but a shepherd, and he was also out numbered, "but GOD"..., hey when 'HE'... wants to encourage and 'Bless' the understanding of 'Purpose' arises with the knowing of 'Promise.' For that one, expectancy can then learn to depend on 'TRUST'. Abram met "THE KING OF SALEM", a... 'MELCHIZEDEK, PRIEST' of 'GOD, MOST HIGH'... Abram's "tithe" was everything, he kept nothing for himself. The king asked for the persons "saved" and allowed Abram to keep the goods acquired, but Abram agreed to only keep his people and the young men from that quantity "saved." He performed the righteous deed and sought no reward, showing great value for human life and quality of living but not materialism. Therefore, 'THE LORD HOLY FATHER GOD'…, soon after made a 'COVENANT' with Abram, to be a "Father" of nations, to 'BLESS' him in being exceedingly fruitful, prosperous, as an everlasting 'COVENANT' also with his descendants, Genesis 17. In the beginning of their "Relationship," Genesis 12, 'THE LORD GOD,' "Promised" to 'BLESS'… Abram, so that he will become 'THE BLESSING' unto others, all the families of the earth. Genesis 17, the 'COVENANT'… completed the vision of "Purpose," that the 'LORD GOD'… bestowed upon Abram and established him, as a "New Man," in changing his name to Abraham. An everlasting 'COVENANT'… throughout all the future generations, "Promise, that is here for us today. Abraham was known for establishing events by building an 'ALTAR'… This was representational and symbolic; to be eternal, foundation of religion for his household being established 'IN THE LORD'. Now in Genesis 18 we see 'GOD'…, visiting Abraham, having been 'COVENANTED'…., and confirmed as a, "New Man" with "New Name". 'THE HOLY FATHER'… establishes someone in all newness "completely"!

'GOD'… spoke personally through an 'ANGEL'… with two other 'ANGELS' the text refers to "They said" and "He said" Genesis18:5, 9, 10 and "THE LORD SAID", Genesis18:13, 17, see Genesis18:1 'GOD'… encouraged relations with him, even allowed him to negotiate, for Sodom's pending destruction! This is personal, "father to son" type of human relations, very special.

Abraham is informed of his family to come, a "son" from him and his wife, an 'heir' and a great nation, from his descendants, to become a 'BLESSING' to all the nations of the Earth! Wow again from one hopeless future, to another extreme. We need to get our own life to "stand" in a position, place, such as Abraham. You see, he kept desiring to "Abide, dwell Live" IN THE PRESENCE OF GOD'.... and fulfil the re-establishing of 'THE EDEN EXPERIENCE'...! Reference Genesis 18:18, 19.

"For 'I' have "known" him, in order that he may, 'Command' his children and his household after him, that they keep 'THE WAYS'... of 'THE LORD'...., to do righteousness and justice" 'Purpose' in the "faith" to be "promising"! The importance of the "Promise to Abraham is established in 'GOD'... 'THE SON'... 'JESUS THE CHRIST'... today, mentioned in Galatians 3:8, 10, 13, 14. 'CHRIST'... has redeemed us from the curse of the 'Law,' having become a curse for us, (for it is written, that cursed is anyone who hangs on a tree), that 'THE BLESSING' of Abraham might come upon the Gentiles, 'IN CHRIST JESUS'... that we might receive 'THE PROMISE'... of the 'HOLY SPIRIT'... through Faith.

Where do you "Stand"?

In another, account of 'THE ABIDING' being offered, the people "failed" to receive it, so 'HOLY FATHER GOD'... imparted a "Blessing" to Moses, and seventy elders who wanted the "experience" The arrangement was prepared for 'THE PEOPLE OF GOD'... to meet and 'COMMUNE'... with 'HIM..., to have the 'experience,' of personal, intimate relations. Exodus Chapter 19 Here we see another man with whom the 'LORD'... spoke and "COMMUNED"... the people agreed to do as was 'Commanded', Exodus 19:5-9, 8 'GOD THE FATHER'... made 'HIS PRESENCE' established at Mount Sinai, and as 'HE'... descended amidst thick billows of smoke, 'FIRE' engulfed the mountain and it quake. 'GOD'S VOICE' spoke to Moses, but the people, stood afar off and told Moses, you speak with 'GOD'..., then tell us what 'HE'... 'says'! Disappointing, they did not wait, to show 'faith' 'Trust', for the beginning of personal, intimate 'LIVING RELATIONS'... Exodus 20:19.

Moses was then allowed to bring seventy of the elders, and priests for an 'experience'..., and they saw, 'GOD,' in 'THE SPIRIT'..., 'HIS GLORY'..., the place of where 'HIS FEET' were, was like 'THE HEAVENS'.... in all its clarity, like a work of luminous sapphire stone. They had 'COMMUNION'..., and 'DINED IN THE PRESENCE OF GOD'... when Moses went up to meet with 'HOLY FATHER GOD'..., a 'CLOUD' covered the mountain, and 'THE GLORY OF GOD' rested upon it Exodus 24:9, 10. The 'CLOUD OF GLORY'.... to the elders and priests, was seen amidst an amazing 'Fire' around and upon the entire mountain.

The great 'BLESSING'..., for Moses was that he intended to spend maybe a day with 'THE LORD GOD'... but that continued into a few days, then more and more days, seven became fourteen then twenty-one, until forty days and nights! 'THE ABIDING'... will change him for life, imagine all that time, day after day, what an 'experience' He "entered into" 'THE FIRE'...! The people rejected, but Moses entered 'IN'... It is here that he was given the mandate to re-establish 'COMMUNION'..., that 'THE PRESENCE'... may "ABIDE", so a habitation was planned.

"Let them make for 'ME'... a 'SANTUARY'... that 'I' may "Dwell" among them" reference Exodus 25:8.

The construction of a special tent was established called... 'THE TABERNACLE'... of 'MEETING, CONGREGATION'... The 'TABERNACLE'... had the 'CLOUD OF GLORY'... rest above 'IT'..., a symbolic expression of 'COMMUNION'..., 'THE ABIDING PRESENCE'... They 'experienced' a 'CLOUD'... by day, and pillar of 'FIRE'... by night! Exodus 40:34-38. This 'CLOUD'... mediated their travels for them, when 'IT'... was taken up; they travelled on their journeys, but when it rested upon 'THE TABERNACLE'... they stayed. "THE ABIDING"...!

Many generations later, King Solomon, built a permanent 'TABERNACLE'..., 'THE HOUSE OF GOD'... out of stone, and the 'CLOUD OF GLORY' also was a representation of the powerful 'PRESENCE OF GOD'... for them. They could not stand in... 'THE PRESENCE'... 2 Chronicles 5:13, 14, and 7:1, 2, 3. So great was their ceremony for the dedication of "THE TEMPLE'..., the desire to be in 'HOLY COMMUNION'..., that they "Prayed" for that active 'Relationship.' King Solomon established a 'COVENANT' with 'THE LORD GOD,' 'SOVERIGN ALMIGHTY'..., in very specific requests. Reference 2 Chronicles 6:20... "that 'YOUR EYES'... be opened towards this 'TEMPLE' day and night, where 'YOU' said 'YOU' will put 'YOUR NAME'..., that 'You' will hear the prayers that your servant makes." Solomon interceded on behalf of the people of 'GOD'... The 'SACRIFICE OFFERING' consisted of twenty-two thousand bulls, one hundred and twenty thousand sheep, when the 'PRESENCE OF GOD'... manifested in 'THE TABERNACLE OF THE TEMPLE'..., even the PRIESTS could not enter, because the "GLORY OF THE LORD GOD'... filled it, too powerful to enter then, 'THE FIRE'...! "FIRE"... was a prime element of action, when Solomon offered the "SACRIFICE'... unto 'GOD.' Moses also could not enter THE TABERNACLE, when 'THE GLORY OF GOD'... filled 'IT'!

The 'GLORY OF GOD'... identifies 'THE PRESENCE OF GOD'... being active for a purpose, ready to perform some function, accomplish an objective. Haggai, the Prophet, declared that 'THE GLORY'... of this time, referred to then as the "Latter day TEMPLE GLORY" must surpass that of their time, the "former day" 'TEMPLE

GLORY'... we should expect therefore to surpass any other experiences of content that ever were witnessed before or even imagined!

You should be seeking to find the place that will allow you to 'Enter In'! The place of 'FIRE'... fall! "Sublime"

Remember.........

"If you... "Abide"... 'IN'... 'CHRIST JESUS'... certainly by 'Abiding' 'IN'..., 'HIS WORD'... you shall ask and it shall be done, you will know 'THE TRUTH'... and be 'Free' to do all things, for nothing is impossible with 'GOD'...! Genesis 18:14 To Abraham, 'FATHER GOD'... declared, "Is anything too hard for 'THE LORD'"...?

A man, walked on the ocean to meet 'JESUS THE CHRIST'..., because he 'knew' 'JESUS'..., and the 'Abiding Relations'! 'JESUS... THE CHRIST'..., 'Raised' the dead, back into 'Life', Lazarus was already decomposing, a break down of cells into decaying matter but nerves, blood, organs pumped back into 'Life', because THE FIRE'... "RESURRECTION POWER"!

Do not allow the limits set by the lifestyles of the world, set limits for you...; 'IN CHRIST'... is... 'THE LIFE'...

"'I AM'... 'THE RESURRECTION'... and.... 'THE LIFE'..."

John 11:25....

One cannot appreciate being "Saved" unless one realises, that he or she was lost and endangered! Many, many do not "know" where they should be, not having the "experience" of such and unable to get 'faith' to "transform" them. Baggage, internally has to be dropped, the inside gutted out as in a complete house renovation. If not removed and refitted, the journey is long, hard, burdensome and treacherous! 'FAITH'... is the ability, characteristic to "Trust" completely. It is difficult to work towards a lifestyle that is not "known," because no "experience" has been received in this area. You can "feel" and begin interaction, exchange, releasing, 'receiving', the New Way, 'THE TRUTH'... and 'THE LIFE'..., 'IN HIM'... 'CHRIST JESUS'... "THE ENCOUNTER" for the 'EDEN EXPERIENCE'... awaits you.

We were made, with the intended 'Purpose,' of "Abiding" 'IN THE PRESENCE'..., that was 'THE EDEN EXPERIENCE'... 'JESUS THE CHRIST'... came to re-establish, through the re-counselling process that the specific design, intention of 'GOD THE FATHER'... will be accomplished 'IN CHRIST JESUS'..., 'IN HIS KNIGDOM'..., here on earth just as 'IT... KINGDOM'..., is established 'IN HEAVEN'!

> Look....................
> Find........................
> 'Enter in'......................
> "In the midst"....!
> 'THE ABIDING PRESENCE'

Remember the Revelation that John revealed, from being close. We can also 'IN THE LORD'... through 'THE LIFE'... of 'THE LIVING WORD'... let it become real. "If you 'Abide' you shall 'Know' and you shall become 'Free' It is for this lifestyle, special relationship with 'THE FATHER'..., that no one, none, except Adam and Eve had experienced! Now 'IN CHRIST JESUS'... as was defined in John 14:21, 23, that 'HE' and 'THE FATHER' will make their 'HOME'... with us and 'HE' will "manifest" 'HIMSELF... to us! This is... 'THE LIFE'...! John 14:6. 'Freedom'! John 8:32

7

BEHOLD.... 'I'..... COME QUICKLY....!

A very important statement was made, by 'JESUS CHRIST'... on 'THE CROSS'... "It is finished"! All that had to be done was accomplished, so it is for us to receive, apply, complete, the "purpose" each one has to fulfil...! As a 'Body' the positive power of unity and agreement can accomplish much, especially with regards to destroying Principalities and Power, every established stronghold of "the enemy"!

'IF'... the works that established the 'Purpose of 'JESUS CHRIST'... on earth, in human form is completed 'IT' is "finished"; 'HE' was not alerting us that 'HIS'... 'Time' was up...! We were informed that 'RESURRECTION POWER'..., would be available on "the third day". He appeared to them, 'HIS' "OWN"..., at their darkest "HOURS"! In their grief, fear, destroyed future existence as 'CHRIST-IANS'..., with 'HIM.' 'JESUS'... 'Entered-in the midst', that the 'PROMISE' not be broken!

The Book 'Revelation of JESUS CHRIST'... is exactly that, the consideration for an end to our world, is a subject no one wants to look at, especially knowing the condition of it and how it ends! Science, Technology and the Scientist who speak of millions of years gone, and the advances in discoveries, invention, produce a false sense of an "eternal life" The world will be served by science. According to

'THE BIBLE'... A.D. was the historic marker, 'THE YEAR OF THE LORD'... and the 'time' B.C. before CHRIST..., was four thousand years, and so far, after A.D. two thousand and fourteen. The genealogies record the generation trace, in the book of Chronicles, back to the Book of Genesis.

However, "IN CHRIST"... one does not have to fear "anything," remember the great fear, is of 'death', which 'HE'... has conquered, and is "UNDER HIS FEET"! 'HE' is our, 'Eternal Life'! 'JESUS CHRIST'... that 'NAME' above all other names, must be fully mentioned, because there are many named "Jesus" especially in the Latin American countries. 'JESUS'..... 'YAHSHUA', in Hebrew, 'Ha Mashiah', 'the Messiah', 'Saviour'

'HE' taught in a simple way, for us to embrace the events with peace and simplicity, that we will see the signs, to inform us of the events that lead up to 'HIS'... 'RETURN'... referred to as, 'The Second Coming of CHRIST'... Just as the season reveals itself in spring time, new buds, leaves on trees again, flowers, fragrance, birds, bees, bugs, colours, stronger, warmer sunlight, a new season of "life", so too will be the changes of the conditions in the world. Then, is when 'HE'... declares, behold "I come quickly" For decades we saw people with written signs "The end is near", but now, faith in science and luxurious lifestyles, entice and encourage us to great standards of living, not seeing the great evil, wickedness that changes even our values, social morals and folkways. Laws today do not help everyone but in fact destroy some lives. For example, if you have fields of corn, and another farmer has a genetic high breed, which is patented. Then you can not grow his breed, the Law protects him. But, if his corn pollen fertilises the plant on your farm, and it produces his breed of corn, then you are treated as a thief, and have to give up your corn if unable to pay legal compensation. Many farmers cannot pay the legal price so have to give up their lands, so one person; one "company" can control all the corn production. You did not dig up his tree and replant it in your farm, and can't dig it up to replant it on his so there is the law at work, in the World.

Back to business, the concern will be, as the 'BIBLE'..., 'WORD OF GOD'... declares, transformation of values, ethics, laws, even Religious values will change! The "presence" of 'HOLINESS'... will be to a great extent replaced by 'Religiousness' causing values of Worldliness and a view to look at great things in the future, and the confidence..., 'THE FAITH'... in 'Man' to solve global problems. Religion will be directed by 'Man' and not 'GOD THE FATHER'.... 'CREATOR..., POSSESSOR'... Alive, Living, 'PRESENCE REVELATION'.... 'IN CHRIST JESUS'... will decrease.

"I will be with you always... even to the end of age." Matthew 28:20, and then there were the 'PROMISES'... John 14:21, 23 to 'MANIFEST HIS PERSON'... to us, personally, and that 'HE'... and 'THE FATHER'... will make their 'Home' with us! The intent, the desire, to provide for us all to come "into" 'ONE'..., 'ONE COMMMUNIOUN'..., to become 'PERFECT'... 'IN ONE'..., John 17:21-23, 25. This is our goal to attain onto, for the "experience" of completeness.

The reality of what is to "come" cannot be seen, until amazing events occur to topple, over-power, transform leadership and institutions, then the unravelling will be soon when nations weaken financially, when threats affect international business, and the internal civil wars cripple nations, then there is the natural disaster that cause damage on a large scale. It takes years for a "people" to regain stability. Eventually problems will be solved when world leaders will be forced to entertain 'Talks' of International Laws, which will facilitate global banking, and eventually a 'One Body Government' for all Nations. Factors, events, have not occurred as yet, but when the circumstances align, it will be the only way.

"THE WAY... THE LIFE... THE TRUTH"... as 'IN CHRIST JESUS'...., will be far from what the world will desire, and the 'BIBLE..., declares that one world leader will eventually emerge. The 'Way' of the world will be "anti-Christ" but seen to the masses as normal, fulfilling, and appropriate as religion becomes "of the people" not 'GOD'. I do not want to go into the politics of the events, but 'Spark' your imagination into the reality of 'FREEDOM IN CHRIST'..., that 'HIS KINGDOM'... should come, be established, on Earth just as 'IT'... 'KINGDOM'... is established 'IN HEAVEN'... so that... 'THE WILL OF GOD'.... 'IN CHRIST'... be done, accomplished, on Earth, in our lives, just as 'IT'... is done 'IN HEAVEN'... This is the 'heart' of the 'LORD'S PRAYER'... for us.

Reference to Acts 17:26, 27, 28, 30, 31 teach us the beginning and the end in an interactive way, that we can jump into the "Lifestyle" and find our 'Position', fulfil 'Purpose' though 'HE' is not far from us, For 'IN HIM'...we live and move and have our being. Truly, the times of ignorance, 'GOD'... overlooked, but now commands all people everywhere to "Repent"... 'HE' has "Appointed" a day on which 'HE'... will "Judge" the world in 'TRUE RIGHTEOUSNESS'... by 'THE MAN'... whom 'HE'... "Ordained." 'HE'... has given assurance of this to all by 'RISING'... 'HIM'... from the dead! Our 'place' is 'IN HIM'... John 5:24, 25, 26, 27, 28, 29, 30, comes from 'JESUS' MOUTH'... 'HIS WORDS'...!

"Most assuredly 'I' say to you, the one who hears... 'MY WORDS'... and "believes" 'IN HIM'... who sent 'ME', has 'Everlasting Life', and shall not come into 'JUDGEMENT'... and has passed from death into 'LIFE'."

Most assuredly, 'I' say 'THE HOUR'... is coming, and now, is when the dead shall 'hear' 'THE VOICE OF THE SON OF GOD'... and those who hear will 'Live'

For 'THE FATHER'... has 'LIFE IN HIMSELF'... so 'HE'... has granted 'THE SON'... to have 'LIFE'.... 'IN HIMSELF'... and has given 'HIM'... "AUTHORITY"... to execute 'JUDGEMENT'... For, 'THE HOUR'... is coming when all who are in the graves will hear this 'VOICE' and come forth – those who have done good, to 'THE RESURRECTION OF LIFE' and those who have done evil to, 'THE RESURRECTION OF CONDEMNATION'.

It is important to understand, what we were directed to 'hear', but we must 'Listen', then understanding and responsibility as expected. Also to recognized the simple saying that one 'Believes' will only be a statement, unless there must be response, action to put into establishment. The mention of "doing good", is not in reference to "righteousness", but to have 'obeyed' instruction, requirements, commands, those who do the opposite of 'obey', create sin then evil is established. Remember Cain, he was told by 'THE LORD, FATHER GOD'.... if you do well, 'good', you will be 'accepted', but if you do not do good, "sin" has already placed itself, before you, and soon enough you will step into "it".

Now, recognize that after four thousand years of "Man" failing with 'GOD THE FATHER'..., 'JESUS CHRIST'... was sent and 'HE'... said "Now is the Hour" for what the Book of Revelation relates, as "The End" and "JUDGEMENT"... Then we have lived two thousand years, after 'CHRIST JESUS'..., It seems that all the accomplishment of "Man",... would be a complete waste to have it all destroyed, come to an end, so we overlook and glorify grand, luxurious, pleasurable lifestyles! When one can "Live Large", then those who are responsible and facilitating, providing, are to be valued highly, even worshiped.

Anyone or thing, that takes all our time, effort, resources, finances, if not 'IN CHRIST...', becomes our God, and is "worshiped". The exalting, lifting up, honouring continuously is what establishes "Worship"

We have already discussed the dangers of "friend with 'THE WORLD'..." the systems of worldliness and the materialism that changes one, 1 John 2:15, 16, James 4:4. Now take a look at Revelation 16:15, ad 18:4.

'JESUS'.... declares coming when none will expect, as a thief moves, bringing sadness for not having been able to protect that which was valuable, precious. Do not go in the way of the masses, especially following religion with general, broad minded attitudes; seek the 'Purity,' the 'Truth,' to be able to stay within 'THE WILL OF GOD, THE FATHER, IN CHRIST JESUS'... Broad is the path to destruction, but narrow, less travelled is the one that leads to 'Salvation.' The entire world is being polluted, contaminated, that all are becoming affected, as a poison that contaminates the air, water, food, everything.

"Come out" otherwise you will share in the sins, and receive the contamination, corruption, destruction..! The 'LORD, FATHER GOD'..., appeals to you, through 'CHRIST JESUS'... to 'check your soul', John 14:30, separate your 'Self', renew your 'soul', do not touch, relate with the "unclean things" and 'HE'... will 'receive' you, be a 'FATHER'... to you! 2 Corinthians 6:17, 18.

Yes, we have to use cell phones and computers, because the world is run on these systems, the TV, communications, but does not have to 'control' your lifestyle. When we start to develop "passions" within lifestyles, then the 'lust, appetites, and finally addictions take control, and all that one can do is "Justified", make excuses, covers up, and also ignore those who contest, accuse, oppose! Not all addictions are noticed, because they seem acceptable and normal in one's lifestyle.

Having spent a year, seeking 'THE ABIDING'… my desires become focused on the "Relations"… that 'GOD IN CHRIST'… was providing, and I asked 'HIM'… for "more time", with 'HIM' not more 'Ministry'! It would seem natural to pursue 'Ministry' but 'GOD'…, who knows everything that I have been through, and brought me back into Provision, Purpose, Place, gave me a "heart" to obtain experience and knowledge, so that I may know and love 'HIM'! 'IN THE ABIDING"…!" For a couple years' business and work seemed to slow down and avoid me, it was a shocking situation, Barely making it for another couple years, I understand, by the revealing from 'CHRIST'… 'IN THE ABIDING'…, that as I become comfortable with accepting my life was not as 'HE'… specified and purposed and when I am "transformed" then become "trustworthy," only then will my stability, reliability be rewarded with a normal life again. It is then I realised that, having no income, allowed me to deepen trust, "know" and 'love' 'HIM.'

I am 'freed'…! 'THE TRUTH' shall make you "free" also; in fact, 'HE'… is 'THE TRUTH…, and 'THE TRUTH…, 'HIM'… 'JESUS' shall make you free, but you 'IN HIS PRESENCE'… 'IN THE TRUTH'… will set yourself "free"! 'HE' will enjoy with you this part of your strength coming from 'HIM'… to do some stuff for your own "person"! I had income appear at times I needed, from sources and people I never expected, I looked forward to the future completely happy and comfortable, working serving with 'HIM'… not paying attention to the results, but working with 'IN'… 'HIM'…!

"But to those who are "self" seeking, and do not obey 'THE TRUTH'…. there is indignation and wrath." Reference Romans 2:8.

"Know 'HIS WILL'… and approve the things that are excellent, being instructed out of 'GOD'S LAW'…" Reference Romans 2:18

Read again Romans 12:1, 2 it is in the "study" of, re-reading, connecting, layering, weaving building and the writing, that the

'BLESSINGS'... lay ! When the 'Word'... is written, it affects the soul not just the mind. Writing more... 'WORD'..., becomes a joy as they come together like family united, or as layers of blocks build a wall, and then, a roof is later laid down, and 'WORD'..., upon 'WORD'...upon 'WORD'... produces a 'SANCTUARY'... for 'THE LORD'... and you, a spiritual 'Sanctuary.'

We had to make notes in our studies, at school, between the text and instructors, our own "record" of what is discovered, known and of value! Today, if we read 'THE WORD', whether occasionally or often, we simply commit to memory. There is a lot of information, to be stored just like in our "personal computer", but who remembers all that was past in it? When you write, not only is it easy to find all that was... personally placed, with personal landmarks, but there is a great joy of discovering things forgotten. The writing makes a very serious impact on your mind, thinking carefully, going it over until finally it is ready to be recorded. Each word is repeated in the mind as it is written; the experience is far more extensive and deep, compared to simply reading and committing to memory. 'JESUS' was called 'RABBAI'... 'TEACHER'... more than any other name by the public.

The 'LORD, FATHER GOD'..., through 'CHRIST JESUS' can come to us and move as fast with us, as we are able to, but it must be according to 'HIS WILL'... In John 15:14, 15 we are simply at peace with 'HIM'..., like children with parents. Only through 'THE ABIDING'... can we move to the place of being treated "personal", and have 'revelation'! Regardless of our emotional or intellectual position, in believing we are close Sons and Daughters. 'HE' still is far from the reality of 'THE TRUTH', but in coming close and staying 'IN HIS TRUTH'... then we can receive 'HIS WORD'..., and the 'BLESSINGS'... in a plan for our entire life, almost like withdrawals from the ATM, being compared to entering the bank vault, to take what is needed.

When I was a 'hot' minded "Religious Christian,' seeking to be more "spiritual", the desire to slip into the flow of 'HIS TRUTH'... was strong. All the times of mid week services, events with guests, foreign Ministries, serving, reading, attending, did not connect me to a "place", that I believed to exist but could not access. When I started to seek an "ALIVE"..., "TRUE, LIVING RELATIONSHIP"... to speak with 'HIM' as if sitting next to 'HIM'..., not casual or as in a passing comment, but seeking conversation then "Relations" began. Full relationship, now was possible. If you do not see someone often or not too interested, relations take long to become established; but if you see value and desire, then relations can be quick. Everyone does have, as they claim, "Relationship" with 'GOD THE FATHER'.... 'IN CHRIST'..., but what type, is not defined. Is it as a child would have or with an acquaintance, friend or a close personal relation? Our emotions usually put us in a fantasy frame of mind, not in touch with the reality of the situation. Eagerness, anxiousness, excitement, are conditions of our emotions..! The working of the "soul" is a much bigger picture. The 'LIVING RELATION' is not necessarily about energy, excitement, accomplishment, but control of feelings, effects of emotions, which is much more than an exchange of ideas, thoughts. 'HIS PRESENCE'... makes you speechless, still frozen, even amazed, overwhelmed, at 'HIS PERSON'...! Humility overcomes and a peace, 'Truth' that silences even the winds, waves, oceans takes control.

The "revealing" comes to us, when 'HE' accepts us securing ourselves in specific places "in relationship." 'JESUS CHRIST....', made the offer, to be with us always, to manifest 'HIS PERSON' for us. 'HE' ever lives to make "Intercession," from whatever condition, the uttermost conditions in which we may be stuck. I remember the days past, when I was having a hard time with life, and the 'WORD'... said 'Great' is your reward in 'HEAVEN.' It seemed hard to accept my situation, conditions, length of time, struggling to then be rewarded when I die and reach to 'HEAVEN'... what about here!

"Love, Grace"... and also a sense of humour, can came from 'HIM'...; the understanding that 'HE'..., has the bank in heaven and I will be able to "withdraw", only as much as I can be responsible with, to fulfil 'GOD'S'... "will and purpose;" 'Transformed to become 'Trustworthy, the ability and responsibility to manage, maintain, that which is to be "entrusted" to you. Start, by considering 'GOD, THE FATHER' and 'JESUS, GOD THE SON'... are 'HOLY', and we must consider, when we 'pray', to become 'Holy', the ability to communicate directly, not in passing comment, echoed statements, letters, text, messages! Enter 'HOLINESS'... in personal Prayer sitting at 'HIS FEET'....! Without 'knowledge', of what our relationship with 'HIM'... should be, and what our character should be like, without, 'THE EDEN EXPERIENCE'... we cannot expect much. 'HOLY'... as was discussed earlier, is a condition of "Purity", of clean hands, pure heart, of purity in righteousness, truth, honesty, love, care, considerateness, compassion. Psalm 24:3, 4, 5, 6, who will ascend to the 'HOLY HILL'..., the high places of communion, and stand in the 'HOLY PLACE'..., not only the Priest, Pastors, Ministries…, but "anyone" who wants to talk, commune, like Moses at the Burning Bush Experience, be 'HOLY'... now! No deceit, no idols, Psalms 24:4, 5 states that one "shall" receive 'THE BLESSING'... from 'THE LORD'..., "shall receive"! 24:6 seek 'HIS FACE'

Let us look at some revealing, Book of Revelation, 3:5 a bit of a shocker to 'know' that one can actually have his or her "Name" removed from 'THE BOOK OF LIFE'..., the one to be opened on 'JUDGEMENT DAY'... Revelation 20:11-15. The ones who feared, respected, obeyed, who meditated, not just read, but studied, contemplated these 'Entered In'... 'ETERNAL LIFE' with the 'LORD GOD, IN JESUS CHRIST'... 'THE ABIDING'... Malachi 3:16.

The hindrances that the enemy prepares come from 'choices,' the matrices, and then the "decisions" we make; in these "last days" many will be 'IN'... "The valley of Decision" down in the Jaws of Life, many will end up in the pits of hell. Look at the amount of loses of life today, each day there are terrible cases and poor sad manner. If we do not use the statistics, and simply use the example of one person in the world, dying pre-minute, that is sixty per hour, one thousand four hundred and forty per day!

Joel, Amos and Haggai, Prophets of 'THE LORD"..., spoke then of what was to occur and now we are experiencing it today. Joel 2:12, 13, we are directed to open our "hearts" to.... 'THE LORD'..., to gather and "hear" from.... 'HIM'... Joel 2:15, 16. Many will be in the "valley of decisions" Joel 3:12, 13 internationally masses will be loosing life. Nations will come to a "Oneness". Haggai 2:7; Revelation 17:13 and Amos 5:21-24, relates 'JUDGEMENT'... coming and the masses will not care for 'THE WORD OF GOD'... through all the materialism and worldly lifestyles. There will be as a "famine" for those who seek the "Pure" uncompromised 'WORD OF GOD'... Amos 8:11, 12. There will be a shaking of all the Nations, 'THE LORD'... also promised to shake "HEAVEN"... as well. Haggai, 2:6, 7 and Hebrews 12:26 for the 'Value of life' will be lost; brother will slay brother, civil wars and crime. "In that "Day", 'HE' will raise up 'THE TABERNACLE'..., the 'HOLY PLACE'.... as it was when established in the days of Kings Solomon, and all of mankind, who are "CALLED"... by 'HIS NAME' ... will be contained... in this 'PURE CHURCH'....! But, remember a "title" without fulfilment of requirements is empty, calling one self "Christian" does not provide 'COVERAGE' and fulfilment of 'Promises'! Reference Amos 9:11, 12. If we look at Joel 3:18, 'THE TITLE' of values as in 'family name' in this case 'HOUSE OF GOD'.... established as 'THE CHURCH'...., will flow with a "Fountain of Purity"! The confirmation lies in Revelation 22:1 "THE RIVER".... 'PURE'...., of 'LIFE GIVING WATER'... flowing from 'THE THRONE OF GOD'.... into our lives, into the 'CHURCHH BODY'... 'IN'..., 'THE HOLY PLACE'....! Who will stand in the 'HOLY PLACE'... that one shall 'receive'! Psalm 24:5.

The 'WILL OF GOD'... 'IN CHRIST JESUS'... is for the "Kingdom" of this world to become 'THE KINGDOM'... of 'HIS CHRIST'..., that the 'Impartation' will be received by as many as possible when 'JESUS, THE CHRIST'... lays 'HIS RIGHT HAND'.... for 'RESURRECTION POWER'.... to flow! Revelation 1:17, 18.

Do you want to sit at 'HIS FEET'..., as Mary to "hear 'HIS WORD'?", and that 'One' thing that is needed, "shall not be taken" from you! Ezekiel 18:30-32 directs us to get a "New Heart", remove "self", for 'GOD'... desires none to perish! 'NEW'... "spirit", for you Ezekiel 36:25-17 One's relationship with 'GOD IN CHRIST JESUS'... is not to be hidden, kept private but become an example for others to "know" what is available. That we all come to 'THE UNITY OF THE FAITH'... such precious treasure must be shared, this is the "Power" for all not "self" again. Caring for others is "Blessed" with ability to help those in need, be a light to those lost especially those who are not aware of their status.

8

ESTABLISHMENT

The structuring of any system that will give strength, stability and security to the public mass can be established through 'THE CHURCH'... The former TABERNACLE... and then TEMLPLE... had a 'HOLY PLACE'... of 'PURE HOLINESS'..., in which only, 'the High Priest' could "enter in" and if he was not "PURE"... in his standing with 'GOD'.., then he will fall dead. Today, we can enter any part of the 'CHURCH BUILDING'... 'HOUSE OF GOD'... that, 'HE'... may COMMUNE... with each and every one. 'HIS GLORY'... of the true 'PRESENCE' is available anytime. The consideration here is "are we ready?" John was ready Revelation 1:17, 18. It is the 'FATHER"... good pleasure to give to us 'THE KINGDOM'..., Luke 12:32, 'HE'... knows our needs, Luke 12:30, 31 in fact, 'HE' has plans for each one and will visit, when we seek for 'HIM'... with our whole 'Heart'...! Jeremiah 29:11-14. 'THE LORD GOD'... 'ABBA FATHER'... wants to be found by us. We can experience 'THE MANIFEST PRESENCE'... ready to fulfil all 'HIS PROMISES'... to secure and ensure all works!

In the stepping out from our "comfort zones," in the moving 'HE'... will move with us, 'HE'... will be "in the midst" of our situation. So we are "Invited,' to come up to 'HIS HOLY PLACE'... 'HIS MOUNTAIN'..., as the same, was rejected at Sinai with Moses. Haggai 1:4, 5, 6, 7, 8 declares that we should consider our ways, this was the warning, if we look to large air conditioned buildings, large screens, and no one walks with their 'BIBLE'..., grandeur and glory of 'Man' will govern 'THE SPIRITUAL HOUSE'; it will lie in "Spiritual" ruins!

Listen...........Listen............Think.

We have received so much from 'THE LORD'... but the shaping, building, even the order of 'THE CHURCH'.... is done by "Man." Much of the "glory is of "Man"! So, the request to come up to 'Mount Zion', that place where 'HEAVEN'... touches Earth, for us to 'ABIDE'... and receive the 'Spiritual tools, Materials' to complete 'HIS SPIRITUAL HOUSE'... is available to us.

Step out, make the move to approach the 'ALTAR'... kneel; sit at 'HIS FEET"..., extend your arms, your heart, and soul. When the leper was told to extend his arms, that was a "time of decision, "Will I be healed or not?" The paralytic was told to stand up, another decision 'time.' "Will I walk, today now?" The blind man was rubbed upon his eyelids with "spit and mud", spit on the man's eyes? Why? He needed to 'know' that his eyes were being tended to, also, the attention of those passing by needed to be gained! "Go wash in the pool of Siloam! The instruction required the 'TRUTH' of 'FAITH'..., when he decided to step out, towards the pool, each step was a faith builder, each one an establisher "knowing' that something was to happen. Maybe he did not 'know' of 'JESUS'... but he stepped out, that walk was the deciding factor not "spit and mud." 'Move', do not sit and wait for a 'MIRACLE.' The paralysed man let down through the roof on a stretcher, chose to be 'Transformed' into a better life. "Healed" or not, he wanted better and 'THE PRESENCE'... of 'JESUS THE CHRIST'... caused him to "receive" that 'CHRIST LIFE'... offered. So having been 'Transformed' into a 'New Soul,' he was then 'Trustworthy' to manage, maintain such and so the 1st 'BLESSING' accessed the 2nd 'BLESSING' to be able to walk. The Reconciled, Transformed mind and soul allowed for another 'BLESSING'… He will not go to the bar for wine, song and women, but to go study the 'WORD OF GOD'… and attend 'SYNAGOGUE'… today it will be 'CHURCH.'

The disciples had been directed by 'LORD, MASTER'… 'JESUS'… to go ahead, to the other side of the lake, they will rejoin together later. They entered the boat, for the journey and encountered difficulty in a storm, taking them into the early part of the morning. They were struggling, the winds, and waves "contrary", against them. It must have been a very tiresome, frustrating time, 'THE PRESENCE OF THE LORD JESUS'… was not with them, because 'HE' was not with them. However, in the midst of their "stormy time" 'HE'… comes to them, in their trouble time, not keeping them away from 'HIM'… any longer. 'JESUS'… walked out onto the ocean to be with them! At first they were afraid, but 'He' comforted them. Peter needed that… 'ABIDING'…, and just called out to be with 'HIM.' 'LORD'… "Permit me to come" and His reply was a simple "COME"…! How many times we are sure in the haste, but to make the "move", we freeze up in spirit? Peter who eventually "denied" 'knowing' 'JESUS', after the arrest finally stepped out and "walked on the water"! Amazing, awesome, magnificent, but when he started to look around at the troubling, pounding waves, the winds and dark clouds taking his eyes off 'THE SAVIOUR'… he started to sink, and cried out "LORD,… save me"! 'JESUS'… reached out and caught his arm and help him back into the boat.

Do we have the 'TRUST'… from living 'IN THE ABIDING'…? They lived with 'JESUS'… three years, yet uncertain about their lives 'IN CHRIST'… We need to "Abide" 'IN HIM'! many are secure in their "emotional," "intellectual," worlds but in reality not as connected as they believe. In a disaster they are shocked beyond repair, 'But GOD'!

"'If' you 'ABIDE IN ME'..., 'MY WORD'...., 'ABIDES'... in you, you will ask, and it "shall be done" for you." John 15:7.

In the Event that you may loose your employment, and home, but someone welcomes you to live in their home, then you must 'Abide', with that one. The values and rules of that one must be respected and fulfilled, you are now in a new "World.". This is still not effective for our 'Transformation', so suppose that one, has to migrate to another country, and you are advised and welcome to join that one and family, to a new land. It is now, that you do not 'know' anyone, no familiar places, can't visit old friends or any family, can't keep in touch with your background, heritage, there is where an 'identity' changes. Complete loss, dependence, disorientation you will become a different character, feel like a new person, new life. This is the 'ABIDING' that needs to be established. "ABIDE IN ME"... for without 'ME'..., you can do nothing"! 'MY KINGDOM'... here on Earth, just as 'It' is 'IN HEAVEN.'

So, many today depend on their personal 'CHRIST-IAN'... evaluation to become fulfilled, but what is their condition on the inside, in the soul? What is your "Relationship" with 'JESUS CHRIST'... according to 'HIS'... evaluation, standard and purpose? It is a tremendous shock, when one seems established, "in Religion" and confident in their 'RELATIONSHIP'... with 'GOD'... but the enemy topples that one's life, after years of apparent stability. Everyone is shocked, but the individual is shattered, emotionally unable to stand for years!

Lets us look at Matthew 25:1-13. A very important message is given, with the representation of 'CHRISTIANS'..., by ten "virgins", the pure, innocent reserved status, is emphasized in front of the more accomplished mature, interactive status. Five were considered "wise", and five were considered "foolish", they were invited to meet "the bridegroom"! The situation seems very specials, unique, at midnight the cry came out to meet the bridegroom. They had taken lamps, but the five foolish ones took no oil supply, just carried there lamps as they were, now asked the wise ones for some of their oil. There was not enough for them all so the foolish ones were advised to go get oil, and while they went, the bridegroom arrived and those who were wise, "ready," went 'IN'... The door was shut. After this, the other virgins came saying "LORD, LORD"... "open to us", but he answered and said "assuredly, I say to you, I do not know you!"

'JESUS'... uses this example to make reference to our status and preparation to be with 'HIM'..., for when 'HE'... returns for 'HIS PURPOSE',... not just 'CHRISTIANS'... by title but... 'TRUE CHRIST-IANS'...! The title is according to 'HIS' evaluation, standards, and understanding. We are "CALLED"..., but not all will "enter in" The times of appointment by 'THE LORD'... are specific and to be regarded, respected. The constant pursuit of fulfilling "needs" causes many to become weary, because they are not ready, not trustworthy, and will miss opportunity, make the wrong decisions. Those who seek "RELATIONSHIP"...., "THE ABIDING"... will be acceptable, be prepared, transformed, and not be "shut out." There was no discussion, for we know how to appeal, beg act, say sorry, but "I do not know you" is exclusive!

It is worthy to note, that many may read this lesson parable, and consider the 'ten virgins" to represent society and the five righteous to be "CHRISTIAN"....! Look, at the first sentence "THE KINGDOM" ... is compared to "Ten Virgins," 'CHRISTIANITY'.... is 'THE KINGDOM'... here on Earth...! Imagine the statistics, if 'THE LORD, SAVIOUR ... JESUS CHRIST'... comes now; "half," "half" will not be 'accepted!' Revelation 19:7, 8, 9; 21:9; 22:17.

"That you walk 'worthy' of 'GOD'..., Who calls you 'INTO HIS'... own 'KINGDOM'... and 'GLORY'!

Remember Matthew 7:21, 23 not everyone who says 'Lord, Lord' shall 'Enter in'!

By..."THE CHRIST, JESUS"... the Life I now live, I Live 'IN HIM'... who 'LOVED'... me and gave... 'HIM SELF'... for me! It is 'IN'... 'THE ABIDING'... through 'HIS WORD'...!

Look..... Listen...
'Study' these, write..., read..., write! Record
"If"... you can "abide"....
"JESUS... THE TRUTH."

'If,' the conditional 'If,' you "Abide" 'IN HIM, HIS WORD', then you "shall" know 'THE TRUTH'... and become "FREED"... Also you will ask and the request 'shall' be done for you. To accomplish this one must be 'Transformed' into the approved 'WILL OF GOD'... for his, her character and purpose in life, through 'THE LIVING WORD'... Become 'ALIVE'...!

Let us look at the how, 'THE WORD'..., could change us for good, reliable, dependable, stable, "trustworthy" character. Turn to Luke 18.18-25

Prepare to "Receive"! Talk "with" 'JESUS'... 'THE CHRIST... as if 'HE'... is your 'LORD'... over your life and 'SAVIOUR... in your life, but you 'IN HIM'... 'IN HIS KINGDOM'...

Most communication is done, hoping one is heard, and we want to believe that 'HE'... hears, and knows all things. Our concern however, is in 'HIS'... "Response", so if we speak as if in one room, and 'HE'..., in another, or at the top of a staircase, or 'HE'... somehow is in a room or space above us, we are not being personal. We speak hoping to be in 'THE ABIDING'…

'IN HIM' is 'THE LIFE'…. 'If' you 'Abide,' you are in 'THE LIFE OF CHRIST'…, then you "shall" experience 'THE TRUTH"…., then become "Free"!

Luke 18:18. A certain, again note "certain," in an attempt to illustrate specifics, certain ruler, in society, asked. 'JESUS'…, what "shall" he do, in order to inherit 'ETERNAL LIFE'…? Notice that he did not want to earn it, maybe get it "free" or purchase it. Probably his resources were "inherited" from his father. So 'JESUS'… asked him if he 'knew' not just 'THE WORD OF GOD'… but 'THE COMMANDMENTS'…, immediately he tried to display "Righteousness", and use 'THE LAW'…, THE COMMANDMENTS'…. to establish 'himself' saying "all these things I have kept from my youth." So, 'JESUS'… went directly, cutting through to the centre of the issue, saying, "You still lack one thing!" Not say what that "thing" was, but got his attention, to teach him!

Then 'JESUS' said, "Sell all that you have, and give to the poor, that you will have "TREASURE"…., 'IN HEAVEN'…" Of course this man will not let go of status, resources, power, could not see what he lacked, because, his life was perfected, all that was missing was just "Eternal Life"! He was "rich", and went away sorrowful, his "Treasure" was here on Earth, not as it could be 'IN HEAVEN"…. He could not "Abide" 'IN THE KINGDOM OF GOD'… here on Earth just as. 'IT'… is established 'IN HEAVEN'… This ruler depended upon his own resources and established status in society being rich and did not know how empty, weak, lost he would be without it all! He should "trust" to put aside all and know that 'GOD IN CHRIST'… will rearrange the perfect life. One is not able to give up or give away all resources, that changes one's world, life. If this one sold all his possessions, lived simple, then he will have a new life. He will be wholesome in relations with people, who he could help and then be valued. He will be able to truly value life. He was not asked to give all to the poor, but to be able to assist more people in genuine need, trustworthy to secure a better 'Life'!

'GOD'S... "WILL"... could not be accomplished, for him. How hard it is to... "Enter In" to 'THE KINGDOM'... here on Earth... 'IN CHRIST JESUS'...! Luke 18:24

The things which are impossible with "man" are possible with 'GOD'! Luke 18:27.

'GOD THE HOLY FATHER'..., made 'COVENANT'... a formal, binding agreement, that compensates using all ones resources. 'BLOOD COVENANT' requires even one's own "life" for accountability. Genesis 12:1-3 can we have 'FAITH' in 'GOD'... as Abraham, did, trusting, experiencing, and seeing in "the spirit" that he was able to talk with 'GOD',... in audible conversation. He did not need anyone or anything else, just 'communion, he lived for 'THE PRESENCE'... trusted 'IT'!

"Get out of your country, from your family, from your father's "house", to a land that 'I' will show you, 'I' will make you a great Nation, 'I' will 'Bless' you, and make your name great." Three "Promises" so far, but the "Forth" 'PROMISE', "You shall be a 'BLESSING'..."

'IN HIM'... we have received 'THE COVENANT BLESSING'... being "heirs" through Abraham, that "in his seed" we shall be also 'BLESSED'...., and become a 'BLLESSING'...! HIS seed was to be a 'BLESSING'... to all Nations of the Earth! Watch, it continues "'I' will 'BLESS"... those who bless you, and 'CURSE'... those who curse you", so that Abraham can stay 'IN THE ABIDING'... and, IN... you, all the families of the Earth, shall be 'BLESSED'! 'BLESSING' upon 'BLESSING', and still more 'BLESSING'...! You just got to give "Praise", and admire the deep desire to 'BLESS'... all "Peoples" everywhere! Abraham was 'BLESSED... greatly, while he was transformed into being, 'THE BLESSING'... But look at the 'Communion' as he talked with 'GOD', right through to Chapters 13, 15, 17, 18, 20, and 22. He was able to do the impossible; no way can a normal man take his only son, and offer him up as a 'SACRIFICE'... unto 'GOD'...! No way but 'IN THE ABIDING'... 'IN THE PERSCENCE'... there is 'Fullness and completeness through 'LIVING RELATIONSHIP!'

Look at the command to leave his family "establishment" his title, support, inheritance, to go to a place that he will be informed of, after he leaves, travels! Go, but not told where, pack up forty to eighty people, all belongings, and not know how long grain, water, supplies will last, what situations may be ahead.

I love when 'GOD, CALLS' out something as if it is existent when yet it is not established.

"'IN' 'THE PRESENCE'... of 'HIM'... whom he 'Believed', 'GOD'... who gives 'Life' to the dead and 'Calls' out those things that do not exist, as though they did." Reference Romans 4:17, 18.

Abraham received from that which was "spoken"! When King Abimelech, took his wife 'GOD' spoke to him saying "You are a dead man!" oh wow, watch out! "Now therefore, restore the man's wife, for he is a 'Prophet', of 'GOD', and he will 'Pray' for you, and you shall live, otherwise 'know' that you shall surely die!" Abraham unknown to himself is a 'PROPHET'! Oh yes, don't you just love it how he was happy with 'COMMUNION'... not title, office, or status.

Notice in the chapters of Genesis all the accounts, how the confidence 'IN GOD' is stirred up ready to burst into 'FIRE'... as 'GOD'... constantly says... "I SHALL"... "I WILL"....., "I WILL"..., shall!

Are you ready to become "ignited within," passionate of 'THE FIRE'... inside of you?

For as many of you as were 'BAPTISED'... 'INTO CHRIST'..., have put on 'CHRIST'... "Self" goes, and 'CHRIST'... takes over

Colossians 2:10. That you will say of our 'GOD'.... "I can do all things through 'CHRIST JESUS'... that strengthen me."

Catch... "FIRE"... Catch it...

All are 'CALLED'..., "YOU" are 'CALLED'... according to 'Your Purpose', Romans 8:28 and 9:17.

"It is for this 'Purpose' that 'I' have 'Raised' you up, that 'MY POWER'... be seen working 'IN' you, and 'MY NAME'.... declared throughout the Nations." That all the peoples of the world, receive relations with 'CHRIST JESUS'... and 'HIS KINGDOM'... be established throughout the earth.

IN 'COVENANT'..., Jeremiah 31:33, 34, confirmed to be "fulfilled," was mention again, Hebrews 8:10-12 "in the midst," of declaring that 'HE'... will be our 'HOLY FATHER GOD'..., and then declaring that our righteous deeds, iniquity, transgression, sins, will be 'FORGIVEN' and forgotten, 'HE' declares that no man will have to teach another, saying. "know" 'GOD', for they all "shall know ME...!" That all shall know 'THE TRUTH'... and experience "freedom" 'IN CHRIST'...

The greatness of "GOD'S"... concern, for us is the ability to seek 'HIM'.... and find and fulfil 'Purpose' this is strongly expressed in the statement to Pharaoh, Exodus 4:22, 23

'THE LORD'... said Israel is... 'HIS'... first born, a Son, so 'HE'... said, let 'HIS SON'... go that he serve 'HIM'... but if pharaoh refuse to let go, indeed, 'HE'... will kill his son, his firstborn. After all the years of persecution as slaves, here comes 'Freedom' but look at how important it is to 'THE FATHER'!

Does it now seem, important, even urgent, for us all to come, "enter in" and "know" 'HIM'..., according to 'HIS'... Understanding standard and purpose?

In Exodus 14:13, 14 'GOD THE FATHER'... said to the people, through Moses, who perform the 'HIGH PRIEST'... and 'PROPHET'... duties, 'GOD'... spoke through him "Do not be afraid, stand still and see 'THE SALAVATION'... of 'THE LORD'... which 'HE' will accomplish for you today, for the Egyptians who you see today, you shall see no more again, forever. 'THE LORD'... will fight for you, and you shall hold your pace."

They had just escaped Pharaoh, and were leaving Egypt, at the red sea, when, Pharaoh decided to pursue them and no escape seemed possible. The 'LORD' also 'MINISTERED'... to King Jehoshaphat, who feared as the Moabites, Ammonites and other 'Peoples' came up upon him for battle. His people prayed, reminding 'GOD'... "ALMIGHTY" of having driven out of the land, the enemies of Israel, and giving it to the, descendants of Abraham, referred to a 'GOD'S FRIEND' forever! They stated that they will stand in front of the 'Temple', "IN... YOUR PRESENCE".., when facing disaster of sword, judgement, pestilence, even famine. Desperation brings people to 'GOD'... unfortunately, and 'HE'... wishes that they do not wait for opposition, affliction, but come immediately, without reason, and receive the purpose of life! These people were going to stand "IN THE PRESENCE"... and not move until 'DELIVERED'... They seek the great "encounter"! Reference 2 Chronicles 20:7, 8, 9 they sought 'HIS PRESENCE'!

But 'GOD'..., 'HE'... just stepped "into the midst" and told them to go look for the enemy the next day, yes, go to them "Do not be afraid, nor dismayed, because of the great multitude, for the battle is not yours, but 'GOD'S'...." This is the confidence we have today that we can stay 'IN'... "THE ABIDING PRESENCE...., not expect it to pass. Today we have 'THE ONE'... sent to us, 'Alive' 'IN SPIRIT'... and 'IN TRUTH'... 'JESUS THE CHRIST'!

"You do not need to fight in this battle but, 'position' yourselves, stand still and see the 'SALVATION' of 'THE LORD', who is with you.

Position your 'self,' having to stand 'IN HIS PRESSENCE'..., full assurance that 'HE' will take care of your situation, if you can stay in 'THE ABIDING'... stay trustworthy, reliable, stable. A new life will sweep over you as a most beautiful "experience" that is unimaginable! This is the teaching in 2 Chronicles 20:17 and 'HIS'... love, delight, expressed in exclamation "Oh Judah and Jerusalem"! Emotions 'IN THE LORD'... is where the 'TRUE PASSION'... is established, flowing to your life, liquid 'FIRE'..., of Life!

Moses and the People of GOD encountered similar situations, where complete disaster was expected as they left Egypt when pharaoh gave in to 'GOD'... but having lost his son hardened his heart. The Israelites at that point of frustration seeing the loss of their freedom in death at the coast of the Red Sea, speak through Moses saying, to not be afraid and stand still, looking at the 'SALVATION'... performed by their 'LORD GOD'... They will never see the enemy again forever! They will hold their peace, as 'THE LORD'... fights for them. Exodus 4:13, 14.

So discover your 'Purpose,' note your condition find your 'Position' and 'Fulfil', become a 'BLESSING'... to others, and all your needs, even those unknown yet to come 'HE'... has prepared for you, 'HE' has 'PROMISED'.... you! Walk into' IT"..., "Enter In" and walk in "IT"... enjoy the experience.

'GOD'... 'THE HOLY FATHER'... told Abraham, to look to the lands before him, and walk in it, wherever his feet go, that land will be given to him as an.. 'INHERITANCE'.... and "his seed" shall populate and own it. Abraham's 'BLESSING'... was not in the future... but the 'now' 'IN THE ABIDING PRESENCE'!

Position your soul. No need for self when abiding in 'THE LORD, FATHER GOD'! When at "One" with 'HIM'... you will be allowed to operate on your own in responsible, purpose accomplishing character.

9

CAPTIVATED......!

The place of peace, balance, stability complete composition comes after one has had 'THE PRESENCE EXPERIENCE'..., then, imagine staying 'IN'... 'THE ABIDING, OF THE PRESENCE'! The being, caught up, or captivated, is where 'HEAVEN'... and Earth specifically "you", become 'ONE'... in 'Communion' 'IN CHRIST JESUS'..., if it could just last on and on, non stop. No phone calls, disturbing or distracting elements "complete composition"

The 'WORD'... that stays in someone, that one will "trust." The one who keeps 'HIS TRUTH'... "Alive" will come to 'know' 'JESUS IS THE TRUTH' and have 'FREEDOM'... So look, those who "Keep" 'THE TRUTH'... may "Enter In" 'THE LORD'S PEACE'... will have perfect peace. The one, whose mind is stayed, fixed on 'YOU'... shall experience 'PERFECT PEACE' of 'THE LORD' Reference Isaiah 26:2, 3, 4.

We identified, the deep desire, to go past all frustration, and seek the "ABIDING"... as we studied the Disciple John and the "Revelation" for him, as we identified 'REVELATION 2' and 'REVEALTION 3'.... experiences of John.

Let us look at another.

REVELATION 4

The 'DISCIPLES'..., after 'THE RESURRECTION' were called 'APOSTLES' the ones "sent" to establish 'THE KINGDOM'... through 'THE CHURCH'..., through Ministry.

Now, the other Disciples, made reference to the amazing spectacular, event, of 'JESUS'.... coming to them, "walking on the ocean"! As with the 'GETHSEMANE EXPERIENCE'..., John was "Captivated", 'IN THE ABIDING'..., and in this event, also was "caught up" in an "experience" that the others did not receive. Many miss the "move" of 'THE LORD'... just like when 'HE' spoke and many heard nothing, some a thunder, and some, a 'VOICE'... unknown!

Let's go to the Gospel, John Chapter 6:15-21 His account, of ... 'JESUS'... "walking on the ocean," is rarely noticed, because of typical human nature, goes to the place of excitement, most action, to be filled with the information that is available. John's "experience" of Gethsemane, Chapter 17, did not dramatise, but gave more information, than one sentence. "Father, not what 'I' will, but what 'YOU WILL'... be done! Great teaching on "self", but most people only receive the image of 'JESUS'... being fearful, facing "Death" upon 'THE CROSS OF CRUCIFICTION'... He was only concerned about the direction of events in 'HIS'... absence. John, Chapter 6, gives the account of having rowed three to four miles out, from one direction, and the wind against them from the other direction 'JESUS' was received into the boat, but wait "something is missing"! What about Peter, one of the brethren who walked out on the ocean to be with 'JESUS'..! Yes, that is tremendous, amazing spectacular! But why will a man in the midst of this 'experience'... not record this 'event', the brother also walked, on water to be with 'JESUS'?

Look............ Look............... "Watch".......!
Revelation

John 6:12, when 'JESUS'... entered the boat, "immediately, straight away" "the boat was at the land, where they were going"! Zap just like that Zap!

"Supernaturally" the boat went through time, through the pull of gravity and shot across the surface unto the shore, where they were going!

Watch....., Look....but...Watch this..!

Some tremendous, amazing, magnificent occurrence must have captivated, taken full control of John's mind that he was overwhelmed, and could not be concerned with Peter, having walked on the ocean! Something of grandeur, colossal, mind blowing effect produced "Captiva", with John's mind.

Look..... Listen...... Think...
...slow down ... "Enter In"...!

'JESUS'..., is sitting on the bow, front part of the boat, as the others are all fidgety, anxious, exasperated over brother Peter's walk on the ocean, in addition to the event of 'THE MASTER' coming to them at that time of desperation, frustration. They were overjoyed at the event, expressing opinions, questioning about it, directing attention to Peter but, John! John was "caught up" deep 'IN THE ABIDING'...... looking at 'JESUS'.... into the depths of 'HIS EYES'... and exposed to events before the foundation of the World and those to still occur. It was a continuum of 'experience', and as he looked in expectation of "ask and it shall be done for you" 'JESUS' took him through "Time" that even gravity stood still, 'IN… TO…' a "Realm" of 'THE KINGDOM'…, here on earth, just as 'IT'… is 'IN HEAVEN'…They went through such a 'Powerful' 'Spiritual' journey' in a "moment of time," that even this World was shaken and they shot across the seas unto land. What an 'EXPERIENCE'…! The others, did not "catch it" they did not enter in! They were "caught up" in their own experience, the event being over but, it is not over until 'THE LORD'… says it's finished! They did not even realise that they did not have to row, to reach the shore! They were not aware of this 'MIRACULOUS'… continuation of the event, that they reached the shore, but how? So are most people, running as if in merriment, when 'THE LORD'… did not conclude did not finish 'HIS PURPOSE'… in their lives. Many times we obtain a "break-through" a 'BLESSING'…. and run off excited, as little children and not receive the "Fullness" or the instruction; many times the full result is cut short.

The term "Bow", of the boat, is in reference to one who sits at the head of the boat, usually the captain of the crew. They have to bow forward, as they row the oars. The oarsmen move forward and their head flops forward in a bow as their body begin to move back, like the rocking of waves to a body. So, the head of the boat is "the Bow", almost as if the one sitting there is being respected in "the bowing"

'JESUS'…, did not seek such, but to create a point of focus for John, as the shape of the boat comes to a point, at the head, and it slightly raised. The back of the boat is wider were the others communed.

John stared into "The Amazing, Awesome, and Magnificent" depths of 'JESUS' EYES'… to "see", as 'He' allows us to 'SEE'…!

Look……. Look……. Watch……!

An example is laid out for us, in John, Chapter 10:9, 10, 11, and 14. 'JESUS' takes care of us, as 'HIS'… own "Sheep" "for they 'know'

His Voice"! 'He' is the good shepherd, "'I' 'know' 'MY' "Sheep" and 'I AM' 'known' by 'MY OWN"....!

"'MY' Sheep" hear "MY VOICE"... and 'I' know them, and they follow 'ME'... 'I'... give them 'ETERNAL LIFE'.... and they shall never perish, neither shall anyone snatch them from 'MY HAND'..." This is a 'PROMISE'.... note the words "know" and "shall" remember, the pivotal "Conditions"... 'If' you 'Abide' 'IN MY WORD'..." you will be as a disciple "and then" you 'Shall' be allowed to 'know' 'THE TRUITH'..., "and then" you 'shall' receive 'FREEDOM'...! Like the other eleven 'DISCIPLES', in the boat, it is so common to "believe" one is as close as possible to 'THE LORD'..., as John was, but in reality, we are far from 'HIM'...

Then you will consider saying the 'PRAYER OF THE LORD' for us, giving "thanks." 'THANK YOU'.... for giving us this day, daily bread, 'THANK YOU'... for 'FORGIVENESS'... as we forgive, 'THANK YOU' for keeping us from "the evil one"!

The enemy comes to attack the sheep, steal away any that can be reached. Lions and wolves, choose a specific animal, then move in on that one, and plan to isolate that one then, take it down. Especially in large flocks or where large animals with strong parents such as buffalo, "but 'GOD'... 'HE'... provided us with a shepherd, who tends to the flocks and account for each one, as his own.

It is for this reason the enemy tries to out smart 'THE CHRISTIAN"... and cause that one to make the wrong 'decisions' become disconnected, as one in the outer limits of the flocks, going in 'self' thinking, to remove areas, and easily "taken down"!

Remember John 15:6, the ones who keep staying outside of 'THE ABIDING'... become withered and end up at the outer limits of 'THE KINGDOM'..., the ones who are troublesome, defiant "self-willed" cannot be "Disciplined" are taken away, removed to the outer parts of

'THE KINGDOM'… in order to make place for those who are worthy and desire to stay within 'THE ABIDING'… John 15:2. The enemy sends out messages to our "spirit," our soul, in an attempt, to lure, entice, "seduce" into the place of "attack".

"We know' that whoever is "Born of GOD…," does not sin; the one who has been "Born of GOD"…, keeps his person, soul, and the wicked one does not touch him, her. We 'know' that we are "OF"… 'GOD'…, and the whole world 'lays' under the 'sway' of 'the wicked one' And we 'know' that the 'SON OF GOD'… has come and has given us an understanding, that we may 'know' 'HIM'… who is 'TRUE'… and we are 'IN HIM'… 'JESUS CHRIST'…" Reference 1 John 5:18 – 20 the 'WORD OF GOD'…tries to teach us "value" for the 'GOSPEL'… is veiled to those who are perishing, whose mind the "God' of this world has "blinded" and not know nor believe 'THE TRUTH'… unless the 'LIGHT'… of 'CHRIST'… shines upon them. Reference 2 Corinthians 4:3, 4.

Reference to Gospel, John 1:12, 13 we have 'IN HIM'…, the "Authority, Right," to become 'Sons, Daughters' of 'GOD', not in title through 'RELIGION'… but "BORN AGAIN"… "REBIRTH"… experience… according to 'HIS WILL'…, in 'BAPTISM' by 'THE HOLY SPITRIT OF GOD'… The disciples had left shore at evening and were in the middle of the sea, at the forth watch, being between 4 to 6 am, reference Matthew 14: 23, 24. They were tried, frustrated and overcome with fear at the appearance of their 'LORD, MASTER'… walking on the ocean! Peter was able to go out and walk on the water to meet 'JESUS'… what an event, wow! 'HE' came to them at their time of need, beyond the limits of this world, changing time, gravity, "translating" them into 'HIS KINGDOM'… reference Colossians 1:3.

So, to be caught up in the "HOLY SPIRIT REALM," slowly slip into "Captiva" and lull, bask, like when one dives into water, and go under, then the body will level off, a wonderful moment to try for floatation, like a bird, fish, not affected by gravity. It is interesting while swimming in certain humid conditions, when the air is still, the temperature of the air being the same as the water. If you roll over it becomes difficult to feel the difference of both gas and liquid bodies, except for the lapping wave action as flesh moves from one through the other! Floatation, suspended as if without time, a unique balance of peace.

In 'HIM'..., 'HIS KINGDOM'... abide with the "experience" as John did, beyond this world.

Isaiah the prophet experienced being 'high' and "lifted up" in the 'Spiritual Realm' of 'THE KINGDOM OF GOD'..., as John did on 'THE LORD'S DAY'..., the book of Revelation chapter 1. Isaiah, in chapter 6, was also able to enter 'IN'... to the place of 'THE THRONE'..., experiencing the grandeur and extensive flow of the 'LORD'S GLORY'... with 'HIS ROBE' streaming and filling the entire 'TEMPLE'... Tremendous, Spectacular, Magnificent... covering every place in 'THE TEMPLE'... by the train of 'THE ROBE'! The 'SERAPHIM'... "ANGELS"... wrapped their feet in wings and face with two wings crying to each other, in extreme passion, at the sight of 'THE LORD GOD'S PURE, HOLY'... entity and character, to great an experience for them to bear. They shuddered and they cried out in respect to what they witnessed, "HOLY... HOLY... HOLY'... is 'THE LORD'...." The doors and posts of 'THE TEMPLE' were shaken, as they "cried out" and the 'Temple' was filled with smoke of 'THE GLORY'! PURE... 'POWER'... 'GLORY'.... 'THE PRESENCE'... causing every molecules of one body, every atom to oscillate, vibrate! Every part of the body will experience this and come 'ALIVE'... even dry bones! The body of a dead man became "alive," when it came into contact with "bones" of a deceased Prophet of 'THE LORD'!

When Isaiah, was able to settle his soul and respond, he understood how impure human nature was and his mind, entire life became "undone" of this world which was in conflict with 'THE KINGDOM OF GOD'....!

In becoming 'ONE'... with 'THE PURE SOURCE'... of 'HOLINESS, IN GOD'..., one will experience pure "worship." The lips will stop speaking, expressing, the experience of pure "Worship," music, singing will become as one, transformation of this world's realm will allow awareness of one's existence, but unable to think! Just "be"! You will become 'The worship.' The closer one gets "to" 'THE LORD'... in prayer, the less words one use, process also come to a halt. 'He' is everything, we are overwhelmed, amazed, stunned! To enjoy is all that is left, this is the "Captiva"! A joy comfort of never being a captive, but held in place to "receive"! Completeness as was the original specific design.

The 'LORD' advised us to "Humble" ourselves, in 'HIS PRESENCE'..., and 'HE' will lift us up before "Men", in their presence.

Life at, L'Anse Noir, Toco, at the Zagaya Mountain region, so high up, you overlook all other mountain peaks, for a distance, the sky, horizon, ocean, all are shades of blue gray. So, isolated, no life form seen, only trails, bark markings where porcupine, peccary, deer, anteater pass and engage in scratching, rubbing of the tree trunk. The lone evening birds pluck out a high pitched sound. Bare feet walking, amidst the track from the camp, transcend a direct link to "Nature" to the "Creator"! The coasts bear the pounding of surf and cliffs, smell, taste, overshadowed by tall trees in a saintly, "Heavenly" gesture. As if the preparation for a 'VOICE'... from 'HEAVEN'... to bring closure to a journey. To 'know' 'THE EDEN EXPERIENCE'..., and the "Intended purpose of life" specific in design, for 'THE ABIDING'!

10

THE CENTRE....

In establishing a "Camp", the chosen place of dwelling, a "perimeter" has to be established for the chosen segment, to be one's own personal "domain", becoming responsible for this plot of land. Identifying landmarks of that "place", access tracks to different points of "egress" all radiate back to "The Centre" of the camp site. We put ourselves at the centre of 'Life', and look out at life, but wisdom inform us, that it is of value to look at one's own "Life" as seen by others, and learn "reality" not "self-impression". Likewise in the layout of the immediate "dwelling" plan, where to sleep, cook, sit, it will be of value to go to the perimeter, the access tracks and observe what is noticeable, to others who come upon your encampment. "Safety' features that work in one's own interest, become of prime importance. The 'BIBLE'... teaches; do unto others, as you have them do unto you, so see others also, as they see you! Learn from others points of view.

So, if we seek 'THE CREATOR'... of Life, Heaven and Earth, then we may learn a great deal, about our own "person" as 'HE REVEALS'! We also will learn, 'HIS'... "VIEWS" on how to exist, live and operate, to our own benefit. Proverb, 3:5, 6. "Trust 'IN THE LORD'... with all your heart," not some, all; we often think all is engaged, exposed, but in reality only some; "Do not lean on your own, understanding" lean on the understanding of 'THE LORD'..., 'CREATOR'..... "POSSESSOR"..., "in all your ways, acknowledge 'HIM'"'... in sitting up, opening the door, looking at the weather, washing face, brushing teeth, in all your ways! Then 'HE'... will direct your path, of your life.

Trust and Depend for Every aspect of Life. That covers everything which concerns us!

"It shall, come to pass, that before they call, 'I' will answer; and while they are still speaking, 'I' will listen" Isaiah 65:24. You will seek 'THE ABIDING'... and call out, 'THE LORD'... will answer "Here 'I AM'"! Isaiah 58:9. Imagine the desire, to commune with you! So take the time not just after a phone call, or TV, just take a moment to relax, clean, clear, empty the mind give "full attention", then 'enter in' to 'THE ABIDING'!

Just think, after "Creating" the Earth, and everything, taking six days, to do it carefully, enjoy each stage, each detail, then to sit with 'HIS'... "Earthly Son", Adam and teach him, enjoy him trying to "name" the animals! Ha! Genesis 2:19. To seek that special time, condition, place to meet, Son, Daughter, Genesis 3:8, have 'COMMUNION,' hear their thoughts, offer Earthly Fatherhood. "In the cool of the day" important, even critical times "in the midst"! Always 'IN'... for our benefit. In their "Separation" from 'THE ABIDING'... in confusion, fear, realising they were exposed too much, above their level, they hid. "Where are they?" 'THE FATHER'... knew which bush, but "where are you in "Relations" with 'ME'?

'THE VOICE'... that once spoke out, after six days, "Creating", 'THE HEAVENS'... Earth, laying down mountains, valleys, vegetation, oceans, climatic conditions, zones, that 'VOICE'... is calling out to you 'HE'... want to "Commune" with you, at the centre of everything that place of 'ONENESS'...! Those animal species, knowing when death is near, go off to some lonely spot, to experience peace, departure. The

Zagaya Crab is able to defy gravity, and stay inverted, clasped to a rock's underside, as long as is needed. It's markings are wavy striations of dark brownish purple and when one dies, it cleaves onto a rock, out of the reach of birds, and the waves, and after a few days, it dries up, becoming a brilliant white and red striation. It is easy to think that this crab is alive, just sitting there, but he stays there, like a statue, no life. We do not have to go through such lonely experiences, 'IN THE LORD'..., even a painful, crude situation, will not be felt; we will be "Caught up" before the moment. 'IN HIS PRESENCE'... 'THE ABIDING'..., nothing can compare, oh what a shame for 'Man' to go through life, and not 'know' "the experience"!

When Apostle, Steven, was stoned to death, he did not feel a rock, nor see it coming, no pain, but "caught up", his face shining 'IN THE GLORY' of 'THE LORD'S PRESENCE'! He saw 'JESUS'... 'THE CHRIST'... "Standing," to receive him. Standing at 'HIS THRONE SEAT'...! The 'WORD OF GOD"... declares, he fell asleep, that is different form being beaten, busted by rocks, falling, slowly dying! His spirit left before the destruction.

"JESUS"... the same, yesterday, today, "now", and forever, "calls" out to your soul, regardless of status. Regardless of lifestyles, age, wisdom, just for you and 'HIM'... to "experience" 'ONENESS'... John 17:21-23. To know 'THE TRUTH'...

The Life Experience, noteworthy, even if one has many resources, finances, education will be filling, but never "complete, unless one "knows" his, her, 'Purpose'! This fulfils deep, deep down to the centre of the 'soul.' Human nature is always to persevere, pursue try and try again, you will succeed at last, and mistakes are often over looked. We vow to succeed next time and ask. 'GOD THE FATHER'... for provisions, tools, to set out again. Sometimes we are unaware of "justifying self", if challenged by others, even go to "self-preservation." And then no one can touch you! This lifestyle causes us to seek the simple or "justifiable pleasures" but later on the roots for problems, affliction, are set, and go deep and if sprouting up, but become cut down, easily flourish again. We must keep the "centre" of our life, pure, through "discipleship" "IN THE ABIDING"! A disciple is one who seeks training in any subject. If we choose to be 'CHRIST-IAN' disciples, we seek a lifestyle as "The Twelve" they were examples of 'CHRIST-IANS'... not ministry. The choice is there to pursue ministry as one matures.

"Where do wars and fight come from, do they not come from "desires" for pleasure?" This is where conflict occurs, and makes situations become difficult, James 4:1, 2. The network of vast dimension, creates "worlds" within the World, when one comes off the "computer", having scanned through information, then "texting" or "calling" someone, then back into information it is impossible to then, sit and pray effectively! Then, our attempt to 'Commune' with 'GOD'... is not effective and cannot be expected to be successful. In 'HIS PRESENCE'... we will respect 'HIS'... "Awesome, Precedential and Presidential" character, but then the reminder of 'HIS LOVE'..., silences our insides; we can willingly surrender to this 'LOVE'... "You ask and do not receive, because you ask amiss" reference James 4:3. All the relations to the world and "self" can cause 'pleasure' to override, and take the place of "Precedential Relations"! 'IN...HIS PRESENCE'... there is "Fullness"...! Psalm 16:11.

Let 'JESUS THE CHRIST'... come into the centre, of your life, soul, and allow your "person" to go into the centre of 'HIS LIFE' and 'KINGDOM'..., here on Earth, just as 'IT'... is, 'IN HEAVEN'! Do not limit the opportunity with 'HIM'... for you 'IN HIM' the one, who "made you" 'IN THE PRESENCE' of 'GOD, THE FATHER'... 'LIVING RELATIONS, ALIVE'

It is amazing, the number of examples, the situations we have overcome, for years lived stable lives, and then one day, suddenly, one is shocked to feel the it all slide away, past, gone in one experience, event! The mind of the soul, can collect and obtain so much information, like a bedroom with all kinds of things thrown around, some under the bed, stacks of stuff, so we need to clean out, removing the dangers, threats in our midst. Remember, "OLD THINGS'... 'die' pass way, and 'all' "Things," 'all,' made 'NEW!' Some other new things are added to make new arrangement, new structure, New Body. Soul!

Two thousand years, 'JESUS THE CHRIST'... came, to give us 'THE KINGDOM' and teach, lead, guide us "IN TO"... 'THE TRUTH'! Then 'HE'... physically left us, but through 'THE HOLY SPIRIT'... manifests 'HIS PERSON'... with us. We can talk to 'HIM'... and 'THE FATHER'... through 'HIM'... all day, every day. This is the event of 'PENTECOST'... Acts, Chapter 2, 3, 4, you don't have to wait on anyone to pray for you, or intercede, you call out, and 'know' that 'HE'... is near to you! 'THE ABIDING PRESENCE'... Romans 8:34; Hebrews 7:24, 25; 9:24 Arriving at the centre of "life" not just your world life, in 'HIS LIFE' and 'KINGDOM' caught up with 'HIM, THE CHRIST'... 'In the Midst' is complete knowledge, understanding, Truth. John in the boat focused on that "Abiding Presence" a choice as the others chose to stay amongst themselves, while respecting 'JESUS' PRESENCE.' A decision was made by John to go further, not fear, doubt and be amazed, but connect to be complete filled with 'THE CHRIST'... perfect in one. This is "the Centre"!

Whenever someone was 'DELIVERED'..., whether it was from a mental situation, or physical as in a 'Healing' from sickness, that one can now be able to walk again, to have sight, or disease removed, that one can go out, work, earn have a life! The 'BLESSING'... produces opportunity for one to obtain a completely 'New Life' not just a

'DELIVERANCE'. In the family of Lazarus, Martha and Mary, 'Jesus' was the 'centre' of their lives, a personal friend. It was sad through his condition worsened, Lazarus had "Trust", in 'JESUS'..., but he 'died'! 'JESUS'... being a friend did not arrive; Martha and Mary, were terribly saddened, and all their friends distraught. When four days had passed then 'JESUS'... arrived and in John Chapter 11, we can see how saddened the sisters, Martha and Mary had become. Mary at home, not going anywhere, Martha went out to meet 'HIM'... 'LORD'... "If," that "if" again. "If you had been here, my brother would have not died!" Reference John 11:21. Martha then said that she "knows" even then, that whatever, 'JESUS'... asks 'GOD'... for; it will be given, keeping open and hopeful. So, 'JESUS'... replied, "Your brother will 'Rise' again!" Not being specific, Martha then played it safe, saying she "knows" that Lazarus will 'Rise' again 'IN THE RESURRECTION'..., on 'THE LAST DAY'... 'THE DAY OF THE LORD'... 'JESUS'... then specified saying that 'HE IS, THE RESURRECTION'... and 'THE LIFE'..., but she said, "Yes 'Lord', I believe 'You' are 'THE CHRIST'..., 'SON OF GOD',... who is to come, 'INTO'... the world, then she went her way. Martha, did not honour 'JESUS' concerns, purpose, her response to 'HIM about 'THE RESURRECTION'... was non-caring and left it all to 'HIM', to do whatever desired and went her way. 'Self' produces 'self-righteousness or 'self-justification or simply non-caring attitudes.

The "PRESENCE"... works for our benefit, to affect us in wisdom, knowledge, changes our course, from actions of "deceiving spirits" that cause us to seek "self will", independent from 'THE HOLY SPIRIT.' Mary, prior to this, sat at 'JESUS' FEET'..., to hear 'HIM'... 'HIS WORD'..., soak in 'HIS PRESENCE...' Martha was too busy through 'self-life,' 'self-pride,' to "connect." She was even convinced that her serving 'HIM'..., justified her to have control, demanding 'HIM'..., to tell Mary to come help. "One thing that was needed" and "it shall not be taken from Mary"! Communion 'IN THE ABIDING PRESENCE'... We have the "Right" to this 'PROMISE'... for our lives also.

Moses, had once become so frustrated, leading the "people" of 'GOD'..., that he could not do it alone, needing someone to assist, and not seeing 'THE WAY'... of 'THE LORD'... So Moses asked "show me now, 'YOUR WAY'... that I may 'know' 'YOU' Reference Exodus 33:12, 13. That was therefore the opening for 'Communion' and the response "'MY PRESENCE'... will go with you, and 'I'... will give you rest." Not just the request granted, but to give Peace, Rest in the soul. Moses then requested to see 'HIS GLORY'... the mighty move of 'THE PRESENCE,' the great "experience" for reassurance, complete fulfilment Exodus 33:18, 19,

"'I' will make all 'MY'... "GOODNESS"..., pass before you and 'I' will proclaim 'THE NAME OF THE LORD'..." "Here is a 'PLACE'... by 'ME'... and you shall stand on the rock."

Later on Moses went up, forty days and nights, unplanned, for he took neither bread nor water, Exodus 34:28. A day turns into three, then seven, then fourteen, twenty one, forty! The unbroken 'Communion'! Try to think of the nature of such an "experience." He went from 'experiencing' 'THE PASSING PRESENCE'... to being at the 'centre' of 'THE ABIDING PRESENCE.'..., he "Entered Into"... that 'PLACE'... of 'THE PRESENCE'...!

Elijah had performed a great task, with the challenge between Jezebel's prophets, serving Baal, and himself representing 'GOD'... They were four hundred and fifty plus another four hundred who serve her personally at "her table." Having given them all day to perform their ceremonies, with no response from their God, Elijah was able to prepare his 'SACRIFICE OFFERING' to 'HOLY GOD, THE FATHER'... and receive the response of 'FIRE'.... that come down consuming the entire 'OFFERING', even the water surrounding it. Proof of 'THE

TRUE LIVING GOD'... through this ceremony to the people, he then gathered the prophets of Baal, and slew them all at the Kishon Brook! 'THE LORD'… also produced rain, after a drought of three years when Elijah prayed, giving him great confidence in 'GOD' working through him. Yet when Jezebel, heard the news, she threaten to let her god do the same to her, if by the next day at that time, she did not do to Elijah, as those who were slain! Elijah ran about eighty miles away, from Samaria to Beersheba in the south, at Judah; left his servant there and then went on further into the wilderness, a day's journey! Talk about going deep to a place of safety, sanctuary, and rest at the 'centre' of all problems. 'THE LORD, GOD'... sent an 'ANGEL' to serve him, food, obtain rest for this soul, then again a second time to feed him, for a forty day journey to 'The MOUNTAIN OF THE LORD'..., Mt. Horeb, at Sinai, see the similarities with Moses?

The 'Lord' spoke to him there, and Elijah explained why he ran, in spite of accomplishing the great "Witness" and establishment of 'THE LORD'S KINGDOM'... among the people. Jezebel scared him he felt alone and sorrowful for the 'PROPHETS' of 'THE LORD'... that Jezebel had ordered to be killed but 'GOD'.... seeing the need for communion, relations said to him, sitting in a cave, to go out and stand on the mountain, before 'THE LORD'..., referring to 'HIS PRESENCE'. As 'THE LORD GOD'... passed by a strong wind ripped into the mountain, and broke rocks into pieces, exhibiting 'THE POWER OF THE PRESENCE' the 'LORD'... was not in the wind then, an earthquake, but 'THE LORD'... was not in it, then a 'FIRE', but 'THE LORD'... was not in the 'FIRE.' Then a still soft, small voice for Elijah! 'MINISTERING'... inside, at the "centre" of all the events and activities and "fears"! At the centre, in the midst of Elijah's situation 'GOD THE FATHER'...expressed great concern for his situations, often referring to coming into the middle, "in the midst" of it all, to 'COMMUNE'...establish 'HIS KINGDOM' and 'LIVING RELATIONS'... for the people.

The prophets Joel, Amos, Haggai were very specific in what 'GOD'... 'THE FATHER'... relates to us concerning "Restoration, Presence, Comfort" and "Living Relations." In Joel 2:25-27 he mentions "restoration" for all that was lost, damage to the soul, never to be afraid or ashamed. Then to be able to identify 'HIS PRESENCE'... "Then you shall know that 'I AM'... in the midst." 'HE' ... is 'THE LORD GOD'... and will pour out 'HIS HOLY SPIRIT'... upon all "flesh" to 'COMMUNE'... to Reconcile, Restore, Perfect. Joel 2:28, coincides with the manifestation of this "PROMISE" accomplished in Acts Chapter 2, through the working of 'JESUS THE CHRIST,' Acts 2:32, 33 'HE'... has poured out the 'HOLY SPIRIT'... who works one to one with our "spirit" in 'RESURRECTION POWER'!

The 'LORD GOD'... had planned through 'CHRIST JESUS'... to flow, "pour" out 'HIS HOLY SPIRIT'....to 'Regenerate, Renew' so that a "New product" will emerge a 'People' in 'COMMUNION' with 'HIM'... personally knowing 'HIM.' The 'SALVATION'... Joel 2:31, 32 harvest separation for 'JUDGEMENT DAY,' Joel 2: 12-14 and provision for restoration, turn to 'HIM'... open your heart, not mind, and reveal the 'soul.' A fountain shall flow from 'THE HOUSE OF GOD'... reference Joel 2:18 and Revelation 22:1.

'JESUS'... will meet you at 'The Centre' and work at the "perfection" of your intended, purposed "Life"! 'He' will use "SPIRITUAL FIRE' to 'BAPTIZED'... and keep an eternal "Fire, Passion" burning within. Remember Luke 24:32..? Did not our heart burn within us?

Look....... Listen....... Feel.......
'THE FIRE'.............!

11

GETHSEMANE..!

Every life is different, lifestyles vary and some individuals have rather high extremes, in their "way", while some are moderate and patient. The quickening of 'The World' has everyone moving, swaying to the rhythms of "the nations." Emotions, respond to change with sensitivity to the environment. If an orchid is taken from a place of comfort, balance, and put in a place with different conditions it will be "trauma" for its existence. Emotions change easily due to our own chemical intake, from products, additives to water, especially food. This stirring of balance produces volatile conditions in the soul and can cause a difficulty in compatibility, co-operation, and eventually distrust. Ideals collide, and contrast, conflict stream throughout life's "seas", separation and isolation results. "Lovers of self", becomes the norm, then "self" feels great as a value and the pleasure of pleasing one's own "self" becomes the greatest of all.

Everyone sooner or later will meet their greatest adversity, challenge, threatening everything of value, "life itself'! Crisis will come to the majority, the rest will have their share of severe... problems, and none will escape. The only "positive factor" in all this is the minimising of such occurrence and the ability to go through, stable and comfortable. 'IN CHRIST JESUS' is the only "Way"! 'THE LORD'... does not desire any to "perish"..., not to suffer... being spiritually broken, emptied or stripped..., to become as nothing..., feeling helpless, worthless cast aside even to death...! It is here that the 'soul'... will eventually "surrender..." and ask... "GOD... help me, take control please..!"

The "crisis" of one's life... becomes, the time to think of... 'JESUS'..., who endured 'HIS GETHSEMANAE'... and... 'THE CROSS'... until it was time to "give up" 'HIS SPIRIT'... to 'HOLY FATHER,GOD'.... 'JESUS,' however is able to 'SAVE'...all from disaster.

Note, please, that... 'HE'... was not in "fear" of Death upon 'THE CROSS' saying to 'THE FATHER' that 'HE' wished there was a way to remove the "suffering", 'HE'... would not seek 'HIS OWN WILL'... but fulfil 'THE WILL OF THE HOLY FATHER GOD'... 'JESUS', THE CHRIST' was concerned about what would become of 'HIS'... "Works," followers, the DISCIPLES and 'CHURCH' to be established as a foundation for 'CHRISTIANITY'...! The comment upon 'THE CROSS'... 'FATHER' why have 'YOU' forsaken 'ME'...? Marked the "breaking" of 'COMMUNION' that 'HE'... had with 'THE FATHER'... during 'HIS' Life on Earth as a "Man"... The "Spiritual" connection was broken, 'HOLY SPIRIT'... removed, causing "Spiritual Death"...! This is why 'CHRIST JESUS'... then told 'THE FATHER'... to "receive"... 'HIS SPIRIT'... and gave up 'HIS LIFE'...

Every time the Apostles' produced great achievement, the enemy "arose" to create confusion, fear, death, destruction, to 'stop' the workings of 'CHRISTIANITY'! Reference Book of Acts

Saul, the Roman citizen and Pharisee become feared, making havoc of 'THE CHURCH'... entering every house, and dragging off men and women to prison. Act 7:3. Then, still breathing threats and murder, against the 'DESCIPLES OF CHRIST'..., sought legal authority to go as far as Damascus, to find any who were of "THE WAY"..., and bring them back to Jerusalem, bound in chains! Acts 9:1, 2, 'JESUS, IN THE SPIRIT'… after 'THE RESURRECTION'… had to stop him and appropriately converted him to 'CHRISTIANITY'! Ha, what a thing! The fastest conversion in history too..! Thinking it was his God, asked if it was 'HIS PRESENCE'… there, and 'JESUS'…, declared it was 'HE'… whom Saul was persecuting, in the people, of CHRISTIANITY… Then the "transformation" due to the Powerful 'PRESENCE' caused him to surrender, saying "LORD, what do 'YOU', want me to do?" Whoa, wow instantly," complete" and watch this, ready to "serve"! Acts 9:3-6 'THE LORD, HOLY FATHER GOD'… through, 'IN CHRIST JESUS', 'GOD THE SON'… has the "Power" to change convert anyone, unlike any other God or Spiritual Power, but we are given opportunity to understand, know and "choose" … 'Life'… 'IN HIM'…!

Gethsemane, was not a place of "fear", for 'THE CHRIST, JESUS'… but in everything 'HE'… gave, the "example" as an appeal to our intellect first, then our emotions! Think about it, this is why 'HE'… was obedient to "THE CROSS"…, 'THE DEATH' by 'CRUCIFICTION'! Philippian 2:5-8

Our "fears" are the concern, of 'HIM'..! Now… having been 'PERFECTED' as 'HIS' fullness existed "in the Beginning", before the "Foundation of the World", 'HE' appears, hair white as wool, not a "man of this world," 'EYES'… as 'FIRE'… cutting through the mind, the conscience, convicting, "spiritually arresting" those in need! 'WORD'… as a 'SWORD'…, cutting down wickedness in high places, Principalities, Powers of evil! 'HE'… is "Ready", to 'ENTER IN'… to this world and complete the mission, "Conquer"! Just waiting, waiting on 'THE WORD'… from 'HOLY FATHER GOD'…! There is preparation, for masses, masses… to come to the "Place" of Restoration, Reconciling, and Salvation! "It is for this 'PURPOSE'…, 'I' came into this world" John 18:38 12:27! Feel 'THE POWER'…, as all of 'HEAVEN'… is ready for 'WORD'.... to release the flood of retribution, reckoning, 'JUSTICE... TRUTH'...!

.......FIRE.......!

There is preparation for those who want to secure there 'SALAVTION'.., in John 14:30, we were warned to "check your own soul"! Where do you stand? Are you in the surety, confirmation of your "place" 'IN THE KINGDOM... here on Earth...?

"Therefore, let him who thinks he 'stands', take head, lest he fall!" 1 Corinthians 10:12

Let none suffer reproach, but keep "Trusting" 'IN THE KINGDOM'... for 'THE SAVIOUR' of all "men", especially those who "Believe", and obey what is required! Ref. 1 Timothy 4:25. If 'GOD' may grant repentance, that they may all know" 'THE TRUTH'... 2 Timothy 2:25 for, "know" this, that in the last days, perilous times will come, 2 Timothy 3:1

God will repay with tribulation, those who trouble you, and give you who are troubled 'rest', when 'THE LORD JESUS CHRIST"... is 'REVEALED'... from 'HEAVEN'..., with 'HIS MIGHTY ANGELS'... 'IN'... flaming 'FIRE'..., in taking vengeance on those who do not "know" 'GOD',.... who do not "obey" 'THE GOSPEL' of our 'LORD JESUS CHRIST"..., they shall be punished with everlasting destruction from 'THE PRESENCE'... of 'THE LORD'! And from 'THE GLORY OF HIS POWER'! Ref. 2 Thessalonians 1:7-9.

Remember, one's name can be "removed" from 'THE BOOK OF LIFE'... Revelation 3:5!

Do not have a Gethsemane, do the 'WILL OF GOD'... in your 'Purpose'... and avoid having to face destruction or death.

Let us look at the "bright side" 'JESUS CHRIST'..., exhibited so much strength, honour, purpose on 'THE CORSS OF CRUCIFICTION'... even while 'HE'... was there still offering "Salvation". There were two convicted men on crosses, at either side of 'HIM'.... Symbolism of two different attitudes when 'MERCY, GRACE, SALVATION'... is being offered. One, not able to receive the 'LOVE OF GOD'..., 'IN CHRIST JESUS'..., did not "trust", to surrender, in spite of the nails of "death". He told 'JESUS'.... to "SAVE"... 'HIMSELF'..., being pressed by anger and guilt, sorrowful from rejection. The other, appealed to 'JESUS', knowing they were guilty, but 'HE'... was innocent, and then turned to 'THE CHRIST, JESUS'..., in surrender not even asking for "SALVATION"... because he was not worthy, but asked to be "remembered"! It is this 'surrender' that can get anyone out from their 'Gethsemane'... this is the final hour for many! 'JESUS'.... informed him that same day, he will be 'IN PARADISE'.... 'WITH HIM'..! PRAISE GOD! In 'HIS PRESENCE'.... no life is too dirty, wicked or evil, but the "LIGHT".... of 'MERCY, TRUTH, and SALVATION'... can 'Transform'... any situation! Just try it. This is the 'FAITH'!

"Wisdom "... will encourage one to evaluate his, her status... with 'CHRIST JESUS'... and not be "self-confident" according to one's own intellect and emotions or opinions based on the standards of others. A "Gethsemane"... is the final ... 'hour'... one experiences before certain death. Anyone imprisoned whether lawfully or unjustly accused, facing life sentence or certain death penalty... can 'TRUST' in 'HIM' who is 'FAITHFUL' and 'TRUE'... 'CHRIST JESUS'...!

Thank 'GOD'... 'IN CHRIST'... for 'Intersession... mediating, for our making of the right decisions...!

There was a leper, he did not run up to 'JESUS'... in hysteria, or pity appeal of emotions, the peaceful moment could be felt, experienced, softly saying, "'LORD'... 'If' you are willing, 'YOU'.., can make me clean." Shortest account of very powerful 'MINISTRY'..... He was saying, that he knew, 'JESUS'... was able to make him, physically and spiritually 'CLEAN'! But if, for any reason, 'JESUS'... choose not to "CLEANSE"... him, that decision will be respectfully accepted! You can't beat that peaceful, acceptance of surrender to 'JESUS WILL'.... It is outstanding, If he had to 'die', a leper, he accepted his "fate; and clearly indicated this, through the pivotal condition... "if"...! This leper accepted his situation, "yes" or "no" he spoke from the place of "surrender". How could 'JESUS'... refuse such submission? 'JESUS'... smiled, at that appeal to find peace, rest, and said "I AM" willing!" and 'Restored"... his body and soul immediately. Praise 'GOD'. The man did not ask to be 'HEALED'... form the place of "surrender" but simply accepted whatever 'JESUS'...proposed...!

Let us come, apart from status, affiliations, association, at "The Simple"... 'PURE TRUTH'.... 'IN CHRIST JESUS'... The 'BIBLE'... calls 'HIM'... 'THE ONE'....WHO IS FAITHFUL' and 'TRUE'.... but we need to "feel" this, not comprehend, assimilate, evaluate, but use your 'heart' and "feel" it...!

Lazarus suffered mentally, not seeing 'JESUS'..., then considering his deteriorating condition. His Gethsemane brought him to death, many are 'DELIVERED'... but he died...! 'JESUS CHRIST' came to 'DELIVER'... Many others who were at the tomb and witnessed 'THE RESURRECTION'...! Lazarus' new body was better than the one that died, even lived much longer than before.

The deep fears, unrealized problems, unmovable stressful situations, cause many to be hardened unable to allow love to do its work in and around their lives.

No one knows when a Gethsemane will become part of their "path in life". Hopeful thinking will focus on not having such a "crisis"... but look at the course of life and condition of the world. JESUS, THE

CHRIST… 'GOD' as 'THE SON'…no longer is 'Son of Man,'… 'SON OF GOD'… but as declared… 'I' and 'THE FATHER'… are 'ONE.' Through our 'HIGH PRIEST'…, 'CHRIST JESUS'…, we can fulfil the intended relationship as was provided in 'THE EDEN EXPERIENCE'… to become 'ONE'… with 'GOD THE FATHER'… through 'JESUS YASHUAH'… John 17:21-23, that we become 'PERFECT IN ONE'… John was "caught up"… at the 'Walking on Ocean Incident', when Brother Peter also walked with 'LORD, MASTER, JESUS'… In the Gethsemane garden, the others were falling asleep; three times, 'JESUS'… had awaken them during an hour of 'Prayer'… 'COMMUNING'…with 'THE FATHER GOD.' Luke recorded such and remembered an 'ANGEL' strengthening 'HIM'… at that intense time. An hour of 'COMMUNION'… not fearful of death, seeking comfort for 'HIS SOUL'… but more, concerned about the 'Disciples'… the followers that will establish our 'CHRISTIANITY'… and 'THE CHURCH'… Chapter 17, the gospel of John is a 'PRAYER'… from the place of Gethsemane, as Chapter 18 specifies leaving that place after having made their 'PRAYER'…

That we would benefit from 'HIS WORD'… and 'TEACHING'… today, reference John17:20 through the descendent MINISTRY of the DISCIPLES who became APOSTLES. The 'PRAYER'… revealed the 'HEART OF GOD,'… IN CHRIST JESUS,'… through 'CHRIST JESUS,'… that we become "United"… IN ONE'… become 'PERFECT IN ONE COMMUNIOON.' Reference John 21 – 23. The intent that the "World" will "know" the 'TRUTH'… as those with 'HIM'…received the 'TRUTH'… John 17:25. This desire of John to seek more and more of the 'COMMUNION'… pursuing that PRESENCE'… kept him alive on the Isle Patmos, to become a 'Revelator'…and die of old age…

Do you think that there was no other way for 'JESUS CHRIST'… to be found and arrested than to have one Disciple fall away seeking the confrontation between HIM and the Sanhedrin, Priest, and Pharisees? Judas would have chosen the path of the other Disciples, but represents the "fall away" mentioned in 1 Thessalonians 2:3-12 and for us today Chapter 2: 13, 14, that all could come to THE TRUTH'... of 'THE GOSPEL'... 'IN CHRIST JESUS'...! The "Call" goes out. It seems beneficial to pursue it as John did with 'THE ABIDING'... to live 'IN THE TRUTH'...

"No fears,"....... never again...!

"No shame,"....... never again...!

"Never alone,"....... never again...!

Come, all, to 'THE UNITY OF THE FAITH'....., let us all agree, that where two or three, gather, and agree, as taking any issue behold says 'THE CHRIST, JESUS'..., "I AM"... 'IN THE MIDST'...." says 'THE CHRIST, JESUS'... "It shall be done".

'THE HOLY ONE OF GOD'..., 'JESUS, YAHSHUA... HA... MASHIAH...' 'MESSIAH, SAVIOUR'! Will not just grant the request, but in the midst 'MINISTERING'... to the soul, binding and bonding the "Believers"... into one 'BODY'...

'THE ONE'... who walks, in the midst of 'THE FIRE'... says, come, "ENTER IN"... 'RESURRECTION POWER'..., TRUTH, PURPOSE, DESTINY!

Liquid "FIRE" flow... 'HOLY SPIRIT'... flow "in me"!

12

PREPARE...... TO ENTER

Trekking through the rugged trail, already having travelled a distance to get to the destination, the bush and shrubs, narrowest of path, sudden turns, one will question, the worth of getting to these "waters" for an ultimate plunge and swim. At first sight, it seems worth the trail, and then reaching down, touching the refresher, at first touch ooh ooh ooooou, its cold! Again, on entering the mind, soul, it still feels cold but it is actually perfect. Overcoming the mind-set, first impressions, we need someone to reveal the "Truths' to us. Once "in", the enjoyable pleasure can go on for a long time, not want to come out. We can overcome disappointments, 'fears', when there is a comfort, a surety for us, the "One" for us is 'JESUS CHRIST'... 'IN HIS ABIDING PROVISION'...

John, stayed close, "knowing" the limitless extent of 'THE KINGDOM... for eyes have not seen, ears have not heard, neither has it entered 'into' the heart of a man, the things 'GOD'... has planned for those who love 'HIM'. Those who, not in words, or thoughts, or the "feelings" but through actions, response, to have a connection, "Communion" with 'HIM'..., 'Trust' and 'Obey.' "ABIDING IN HIS LOVE"... is illustrated in John 15 and the reading of 1 John, Chapters 1-5. John was exiled to the Isle of Patmos, and unlike some of his brethren, who met harsh deaths, he became a "Revelator", and conveyed 'THE KINGDOM OF GOD, IN CHRIST JESUS'..., to us, translated the "WILL OF JESUS"... to us. Revelation 1:17, 18 reveals, for us to "Enter, Receive" "THE RESURRECTION POWER'... to complete our, lives, fulfil the establishment of 'THE CHURCH BODY'...through 'THE KINGDOM'... here on Earth... just as 'IT'... 'KINGDOM'..., is 'IN ... HEAVEN'.....

'JESUS... THE CHRIST'... is our 'COMPLETION'..., Colossians 2:10, we have been 'BLESSED'... with "every" 'SPIRIUAL BLESSING'..., Ephesians 1:3, "Raised" together and made to "sit", 'IN'... HEAVENLY PLACES'... Ephesians 2:6. So, let us look at how stable and secure our 'lifestyle is 'IN JESUS CHRIST'... and affects others, in daily living and overcome the mind-set of thinking patterns that causes many to say, "I know 'GOD'"... "I have 'GOD'"... "GOD is with me"...

We must be 'IN HIM'... 'HIS KINGDOM' come in 'CHRIST JESUS'... on Earth just as 'HIS KINGDOM'... is established 'IN HEAVEN'...so that as we 'Abide' 'IN HIS KINGDOM'... 'HIS WILL'... be done, accomplish in our lives on earth just as 'IT"... 'HIS WILL'... is done 'IN HEAVEN'...!

Daniel, Chapter 2, 3 Having recently entered "captivity", being brought to Babylon, Persia, with three companions, were found to be far greater in wisdom and understanding than all the kings magicians, astrologers. When king Nebuchadnezzar, could not get his magicians, sorcerer or astrologers, to tell him of his own dream, and interpret it, he issued a decree which went out to cause all the wise men of Babylon be killed. Daniel asked to have the Decree stopped, so that he may have to opportunity to fulfil the king's request, and save the wise men of Babylon, his own soul, and companions. Note the use of the words "know, known" Chapter 2:3, 5, 9, 15, 17, 22, 23, 26, 28-30.

Daniel did not present his own person, as a magician or sorcerer, but as having received "Revelation" from 'GOD'... Having accomplish the requirement, the king lay prostate before Daniel, amazed at his "abilities", and demanded he be given a "present", and offering, and declared that his 'GOD', is the 'GOD' of Gods' and "revealer" of secrets. Daniel that day became Chief Administrator over all the "wise men of Babylon", and 'Ruler', over the province of Babylon and that Shadrach, Meshach, Abednego to be positioned, over the affairs of Babylon. Daniel was placed at the gateway of the affairs of the king.

The enemy then came against them, in the worst way, by causing the king, Nebuchadnezzar to erect a statue to be worshipped, approximately ninety feet high, clad in gold. A Decree went on that, whenever worship were made, for the God of Babylon, when the musicians sounded, all people, regardless of nationality, must fall to the ground and worship the statue. Anyone, not obeying, will be immediately thrown into a fiery furnace! At that appointed time of the worship ceremony, these Jews were accused of violating the Decree; the intent was to definitely remove them and then Daniel later from the governmental position.

Shadrach, Meshach, Abednego, were brought before the king's, "presence", and he gave them the opportunity to worship the God statue, or be thrown into the "furnace". The king however, asked them, who is the God, that can 'Deliver' them form his hands!

Well, the three of them informed the king that they did not, have to discuss this matter with him, and that their 'GOD'..., is able to 'Deliver' them, from the furnace "Fire", and also, from the Authority of his hands! And if 'GOD'... decides not to do so, they are at peace with that decision, and will still refuse to serve his Gods or worship the statue. Nebuchadnezzar was too furious, he commanded the worker to make the furnace fire, seven times more heated than the normal. Certain men of valour bound the three, Shadrach, Meshach, Abednego, and cast them into the fire furnace, but the heat was so strong and "Fire" violent, the men of valour were killed.

But GOD'... stood by 'HIS'... people, and caused the King to jump up with utter amazement and surprise saying in haste "Did we not throw the three men bound, into the 'midst' of the "fire"? And received the answer "yes, Oh king."

"Look" he cried not "I see four men "loose" walking in the 'midst' of the "FIRE".... and they are not hurt....... and.......

REVELATION 5

.... and the fourth one looks like 'THE SON OF GOD'..."!!! Wow "PRAISE GOD'! The comment was not that one looks like an 'ANGEL', or 'HOLY MAN'... but the 'SON OF GOD'... whoa...! "REVELATION"...! 'PRESENCE OF GOD, IN CHRIST JESUS'..., way back in that era, the King, not knowledgeable about this kind of information, in Jewish Religion. Where did he get this from? "REVELATION"... time! Imagine that even the workers of the enemy will "know," 'THE PRESENCE'.., and declare 'THE SON OF GOD'...! 'GOD'... 'IN'... The midst of 'HIS'... people! 'GOD'... for us... 'IN THE MIDST'... of anything. If 'HE'... can intervene and give "Revelation"... to the enemy, imagine what 'HE'... can 'REVEAL'... to you.

'GOD'... our 'HEAVENLY FATHER'... is Awesome..!

'JESUS, GOD THE SON'..... yesterday and today. "now," for you, forever, Eternal for you. Through time, throughout history and now for you. 'THE ABIDING PRESENCE'...!

Later on, in the time of king Darius, an attempt was made to have Daniel removed from office, and plan to have him destroyed! Daniel Chapter 6. Daniel was one of three governors, over all the kingdoms, senators; he was distinguished, above the other governors, described as having an "excellent spirit" in him. When nothing could be found possible to lay change against him they sought to be successful, in areas concerning his "GOD"... with whom his "relationship" seemed exceptional.

So the governors and senators, presented to the King, a plan, by all of them and administrators, councillors, advisors, to have established, a Decree, that no one could petition any God or man, for more than thirty days, the King alone must be petitioned in honour, worship, service. The Decree was also, according to their law to be unable, for change to come upon it, not even by the King. When Daniel "knew" of this Decree, he went up to his room, opened the window, towards Jerusalem, and "prayed" to 'GOD'..., giving "Thanks"! So, in time, he was bought up before king Darius, who was so disappointed, saddened, because he was unable to help him and set his "heart" to the works of 'Delivering' Daniel from the "sentencing"!

The Governors and Senators informed the King that he must "know" that the Decree cannot be changed, and Daniel was taken to fulfil the requirement of the Decree, which specified, being thrown into the lion's dungeon! The King, however said through the stirring of 'Faith' for Daniel's safety, because of his outstanding character and lifestyle "Oh Daniel, your 'GOD'... whom you "serve" continually, 'HE'... will 'DELIVER'... you!

Early next morning King Darius arose, and in haste went to the dungeon. "PRAISE GOD"... for 'Righteousness, Mercy and Love, as Darius cried out "Daniel, "servant" of 'THE LIVING GOD'... has your 'GOD'... whom you "serve" continually, been able to 'DELIVER'...

you from the lion dungeon?" Then, the voice of Daniel come back up "Oh King, live forever" encouraging the 'FAITH'... that could change his life! It was stated that Daniel was not injured because he 'Trusted' 'IN'... his 'GOD'...!

That description stands profoundly, "THE LIVING GOD"... whom you 'SERVE' continually... represents the 'CHRISTIAN LIFE'... in 'serving,' assisting others to "find" the 'WAY'... 'TRUTH'... 'LIFE'... 'IN THE KINGDOM'... here on earth, and this is the "REVELATION".... The 'CHRIST-IAN'... lifestyle was represented by 'The Twelve' and others that joined them as a "prototype". In the natural lifestyle, according to the World, it is expected that this lifestyle will be rejected and thus classified as of "those in Ministry"... The majority of "Christian" seek a lifestyle that is based on trying to be 'good,' and do 'good,' to please 'GOD'... to know everything, see everything. "Those of The Way"... "Christ Like Ones," are our standard and the great example, 'IN CHRIST JESUS'... to remove "self" independent lifestyle, habits, thinking patterns, that separate us from 'GOD IN CHRIST'... to become like... 'CHRIST'... The World has corrupted, contaminated 'GOD'S' intended development and now we must re-instate, re-establish' GOD' Lifestyle, Standards, and Values. 'JESUS'... gave up 'HIS LIFE'... 'HIS SELF'... to become "PERFECTED"... that 'PURPOSE'... be completed, this is our example. Reference John 3:3, 5, 7, to become 'Born Again,' as 'New life,' from removal of the Old Life, completely as from death.

The term "serve" produces thoughts of works that may not be attractive and enjoyable, but the lifestyle of 'CHRIST-IANS'... is created around love and sharing. The receiving is always great, but it is better to seek to give, than to seek to receive. The 'point' most missed is that with 'CHRIST'...anything, situation, place will become "delightful" for 'HE'... is 'PERFECT'... and 'HIS KINGDOM'... is the same! 'HIS

PRESENCE'… is an experience that cannot be withheld, 'HIS' works must be shared, the confidence in "ITS" greatness and more to come is overwhelming and causes the desire to share. We do these things, with 'HIM'… and from within 'HIM'… 'HIS POWER'…

REVEALTION 6

'THE KINGDOM OF GOD'… come, be established, here on Earth…

just as 'IT,' 'THE KINGDOM'… is, established 'IN HEAVEN'…!

We can "Enter"… "Experience"… 'THE KINGDOM OF GOD'…, 'HEAVEN'… here on Earth!

We can "abide" "live" 'IN THE KINGDOM OF GOD'… here on Earth, so that 'THE WILL OF GOD, THE FATHER'… be done, accomplished, here on Earth, just as 'IT'… 'WILL OF GOD'… is done 'IN HEAVEN'!

Imagine our parents, grandparents… all valued "THE LORD PRAYER"… for us but, did not 'LIVE IN THE KINGDOM OF GOD'…. 'IN CHRIST JESUS'… as we could today! How many are able to receive this 'PROVISION'… such abiding ability?

…ON Earth.., 'THE KINGDOM OF GOD'…. exactly, just as existing 'IN HEAVEN'…. 'THE THRONE OF GOD'…, ANGELS… all the inhabitants, "POWER"… 'GLORY'

'Living Revelation' for us to… "ENTER IN"… AND "ABIDE"!
ON Earth, just, as it is, 'IN HEAVEN'! Amen.

"Live" for 'THE REVELATION EXPERIENCE'... you will not be able to keep away from... 'THE ABIDING'..., it is provided to be... 'ETERNAL'!

'GOD THE FATHER'... will provide... protect... establish... you.
"IT"... 'IS FINISHED'!

The 'WORKS'... PROVISIONS'... are all put in place, position your life, soul, and 'receive' 'THE INHERITANCE'.... 'IT IS FINISHED'... 'IN CHRIST JESUS'... reference John 19:30.

'JESUS'... was not referring to 'HIS'... time, being finished, no, 'HIS WORKS'... on 'THE CROSS'... for us for you is 'FINISHED'... completed as was intended.

That we may "know" 'THE TRUTH'... and 'FREEDOM... IN CHRIST'..., to come out from the enigma. "FATHER... "FORGIVE".... them, for they do not 'know'" not "know" what they were doing then, and now, two thousand years gone, still do not "know" 'THE TRUTH'! Reference Luke 23:34.

'JESUS'... is 'THE TRUTH'!

"Behold 'I' stand at the door, and knock, "if", anyone hears 'MY VOICE'... and opens the door, 'I WILL,'... come in and 'COMMUNE' with that one, and that one with 'ME'..."

Well, it seems appropriate that 'THE HOLY ONE OF GOD'... 'THE CHRIST, JESUS'... have a say I our lives... don't you agree?

As was said to the DISCIPLES... in 'HIS'... last hours, and they did not realise, the "Hour," of 'HIS'... arrest would be soon!

"'I' still have many things to say to you but, you cannot bear them now." John 16:12.

All people,… all things,… made by 'HIM'… for 'HIM'… without 'HIM'… nothing was made, 'GOD IN CHRIST JESUS'…

But, all things spoken, conveyed, taught by our 'JESUS CHRIST'… comes to one main concern that 'HE'… came to us, for us! HE'… gave 'HIS LIFE'… that we will learn, change, and become ready, stable, secure, trustworthy for 'LIVING RELATIONS…. IN HIM'!

He gave 'HIS LIFE'… that we will learn to also give up the old life, shaped by this world, affected by the enemy; that we become perfected' and fulfil a 'Purpose' planned, specified from the "foundation of this world", not just form "the womb"!

Luke 16:19-31 gives an account, 16:23-26 makes a "Point" of great value. We need to shine the light that others may come 'IN'… 'THE TRUTH'…! Regret, for missing an opportunity to "save" life, is hard on the conscience. That man refused to help the needy before him daily, yet saw an eternity of regret and torment as a result of his "choices."

"Having been 'PERFECTED'… 'JESUS'…. become 'THE AUTHOR' of 'ETERNAL SALVATION'… to all who "obey" 'HIM'…" Hebrew 5:9 and give the 'HOLY SPIRIT' to those who "obey"… Acts 5:32, or the sad result as Romans 2:7, 8, for those who are "self-seeking" receive hardship, wrath, rage… scorn…!

So until, "The kingdom of this world has become, 'THE KINGDOM'… of our 'LORD'… and of 'HIS CHRIST'… and 'HE'… reign forever, and ever." Revelation 11:15 let us 'ARISE'… 'IN'…, 'THE POWER OF HIS RESURRECTION'… and "know" 'HIM'… be "found" 'IN HIM'… Philippians 3:8-11.

We must try to be a 'BLESSING'… to others, as we were 'BLESSED'… to be that 'BLESSING'…, Genesis 12:2, 3. That the world may 'know' 'JESUS, THE CHRIST'… 'LORD' of our lives, 'HIGH PRIEST'… and

'INTERCESSOR'... Hebrew 7:24, 25; 9:29; 2 Timothy 2:5; Romans 8:34; Hebrew 1:2, 3. 'PRAISE GOD'

Nothing happens by chance; all controlled every hair that falls from your head, all "numbered"! Every leaf that falls all directed. DO you think, that the enemy was able to sneak into 'THE EDEN', to tempt, Eve, and Adam without the knowledge of 'GOD'? Of course not, 'THE FATHER'... had them covered all the time, in 'HIS SIGHT'... of course! 'HE' knew time and place, the appropriate time, they had to make decisions, about their" lifestyle, values and choices", maturity was at hand. Time to eat from the 'TREE OF KNOWLEDGE'... was available when they were ready; they failed at staying 'IN THE ABIDING OF HIS LOVE'!

But, thank 'GOD'. For 'JESUS CHRIST'.

'THE RIVER', OF 'LIFE GIVING WATERS'... is flowing, like a liquid fuel so be ready for "THE SPARK".... to ignite the 'Passion Fire", get ready! Revelation 22:1

REVALATION 7

Comes, when you "Enter In' to 'THE ABIDING'....
That specific 'REVEALING... from... within, 'JESUS, CHRIST"... to you alone!

'HE'... walks "in the midst" of 'THE SEVEN FIRES'... to "impart" unto the ones who are ready, to fulfil "Life". Until we all "enter in" to 'purpose' till we all come to the 'UNITY OF THE FAITH'... and grow 'in' all things 'into' 'HIM'....., the fullness of the stature, 'JESUS,

THE CHRIST"... Reference Revelation Chapter 1:10-20; 2:1; Ephesians 4:13-15.

The 'REVEALING'...from within 'HIS PRESENCE'..., 'IN... THE ABIDING'...!

ONE LORD... ONE GOD AND FATHER... ONE SAVIOUR... ONE SPIRIT....... ONE BAPTISM..........

THE LAST WORD

There is one thought, that raises one "question" at this processing and understanding, "Where does one stand with 'THE GOD'...?" If, and the 'condition' is established with the "if," you do your best, in constant pursuit of 'Living Relations'... with 'THE FATHER'... 'IN CHRIST JESUS'... then you will 'Enter In' to "The Fullness." We are so 'Blessed' to have the knowledge and the teaching by 'The Rabbi, Teacher'... 'JESUS'... "Covering" all that we have been exposed to in this pursuit, is the comfort of having 'GOD'... 'SOVERIGN, ALMIGHTY'... present 'HIS PERSON'... for us... as 'FATHER, ABBA'... Romans 8:15, and become 'HEIRS OF INHERITANCE'... see Romans 8:16, 17, and 'CHRIST SPIRIT'... dwells in our hearts, Galatians 4:6.

No other spirits and powers, made into Gods by man can compare to 'THE ONE'... who is 'CREATOR'... to offer so much and so personal in 'LIVING RELATIONS'... It is in the "knowing" 'HIM IN CHRIST JESUS'... 'GOD THE SON'... we speak of 'HIM'... The event of 'JESUS'... walking on the ocean and then Peter being allowed to also go out onto the waters to meet ...'HIM'... opened all the Disciples' minds to the 'KNIGDOM REALM'... and John had 'Entered In'...! On re-entering the boat John sought for more and more connection, with 'CHRIST JESUS'... so it was granted. He did not seek to run with the opportunity, to have more and enjoy, but go where 'THE MASTER, LORD'... will take him. As the others were

enjoying the event … John… was seeking more with 'IN CHRIST'…
He received a "Supernatural" experience, out of this world, greater than
"walking on water"…! What a 'BLESSED'… opportunity.

John was able, being separated from the world, in exile on the
Isle of Patmos, all his brother Disciples gone, life as a prisoner on the
island, but he turned it into 'Sanctuary.' He was … 'Captivated'…
caught up in spirit and had 'Perfect Communion'… up into 'THE
PRESENCE'… with 'THE ABIDING.' The condition of emptiness
on the inside allowed 'CHRIST JESUS'… to "fill" him up and
in the beauty of 'HOLINESS'… John was 'Transformed' in the
spirit and fell at 'JESUS' FEET.' It is at this point of readiness that
'JESUS'… laid 'HIS RIGHT HAND'… upon him and "imparted"
'RESURRECTION POWER'… unto him, to be passed onto us, 'THE
LIVING WORD'… and 'THE HOLY SPIRIT'…Revelation 1:17, 18.
'JESUS'… gives 'HIS TESTIMONY'… of 'RESURRECTION' at
this impartation "'I Am, HE' who LIVES, was dead but behold, 'I
AM'… 'ALIVE'… forever more.

Today, right now, 'JESUS'… is walking "in the midst" of
'THE HOLY FIRE'…seeking the ones who are ready, prepared for
"Transformation," through 'THE RESURRECTION POWER'… see
Philippians 3:7-11.

"'I' came that they will have Life, and more abundantly." This
'BLESSING'… will ensure that we are able to let 'HIS LIGHT'… shine
from our lives and cause many to have opportunity to 'Enter In'… to
'The Unity of The Faith'… It was said of 'HIM'… that all things were
made by 'THE FATHER'… through 'HIM'…No longer limited to
"human" conditions as 'SON OF GOD'… Son of Man, but now 'GOD
'… as 'THE SON'…in 'THE SON'… 'GOD THE SON'… 'JESUS
THE CHRIST'… is now our 'HIGH [RIEST'… and 'MEDIATOR'…
of 'THE HOLY COVENANT'…

Do you want to be closer to the 'ONE'... who made you? Gospel John 1:3, 4, 9; Ephesians 3:9; Colossians 1:16; Hebrews 1:3 'HIS SPIRIT'... gave "spark" to ignite your spirit and life of your soul in the womb. So allow 'HIM'... let 'HIM'... do the work of 'THE BAPTISM'... of 'FIRE"... by the ... 'HOLY SPIRIT'...

In Luke 12:49, 50 'HE'... has a 'FIRE'... to send on the Earth and oh now 'HE"... has it "kindled" and so distressed until the 'BAPTISM'... is completed. That we may 'know'... what is the "Fellowship of The Ministry," which from the beginning of the ages was hidden 'IN GOD'... who Created all things through 'CHRIST JESUS'... to the intent that now, the manifold 'WISDOM OF GOD'... might be made 'known' by 'THE CHURCH'... reference Ephesians 3:9,10. This is possible "according to the 'Eternal Purpose,' which 'HE'... accomplished 'IN CHRIST JESUS'... our 'LORD'... in whom we have boldness and access with confidence, through 'Faith'... 'IN HIM'..." Ephesians 3:11, 12.

The appeal to you this day is to seek 'THE ABIDING PRESENCE'... and allow 'HIM'... who made you to 'COMPLETE'...what the World and its systems took from your heritage and inheritance... to receive the Life and Purpose to have 'THE EDEN EXPERIENCE.'

This is why we sing "IN 'YOUR PRESENCE' that is where I belong. IN 'YOUR PRESENCE'... oh 'LORD'... 'GOD'... seeking 'YOUR FACE'... touching 'YOUR GRACE'... 'IN'... the cleft of 'YOUR HEART'..."

Feel the 'LIFE'... of 'JESUS CHRIST'... cause every molecule of your being to vibrate, flow through you, transforming, adjusting, adding as 'HE'... lays 'HIS RIGHT HAND'... upon your 'Person'... Position your being, get ready, open up, and receive it. Let the 'SPIRIT OF CHRIST'... cause you to cry out, when 'HE'... touches someone, they always cry out. Reference Galatians 4:6. Put on ... 'THE MIND'...

that was in 'JESUS THE CHRIST'... Philippians 2:5 and 'know' that a man is not "justified" by 'his' works, but through the 'FAITH'... that one has 'IN CHRIST'... Galatians 2:16.

Seek for... 'THE PROMISES OF GOD'... through 'IN CHRIST JESUS'...that having "abided"... the manifestation will be fulfilling in your life. That you will ask... and ... "it shall be done for you." John 15:7

Receive... 'THE WAY'...
Utilise... 'THE TRUTH'...
ABIDE... 'IN ...THE LIFE'...

Then you shall bear... 'Fruit'... It will be evident when others come to pick the ... 'Fruit'... Then you will be aware of your ...'Fruit'... which is... 'IN CHRIST'... Then others will partake and go out to bear ...'Fruit'... of their own... Then we will all come to ...'THE UNITY OF THE FAITH'... Ephesians 4:13-16.

'FREEDOM'........'IN JESUS THE CHRIST'
John 14:6;
8:31, 32.

A ...'PURE RIVER'... of... 'WATER OF LIFE'... clear as crystal, proceeding from... 'THE THRONE OF GOD'... and of... 'THE CHRIST'... reference Revelation 22:1.

"If"... you... 'ABIDE'...!

"'I' 'JESUS'… have sent 'MY ANGEL'… to Testify these things, to you, 'IN THE CHURCHES'…." Revelation 22:16.

Behold, when you see the signs. "'I' come quickly!" Revelation 22:7; 12, 20.

The one who is unjust, let him, her, be unjust still, the one who is filthy, let that one be filthy still, the one who is righteous, let that one be righteous still, the one who is HOLY, let that one be holy still Revelation 22:11

And… 'THE SPIRIT' and 'THE BRIDE'… say 'Come', and let anyone who thirst, "Come", whoever desires, let that one take of 'THE WATER OF LIFE'… freely! Revelation 22:17

FREEDOM…. IN CHRIST JESUS…! Amen.

"Now, 'SALVATION'.... and 'STRENGTH' and......
'THE KINGDOM'.... of our.... 'GOD'... and
'THE POWER' of....'HIS CHRIST'... have come
....for the accuser of our brethren, who accused them...
before our... 'GOD'... day and night, has been....
"cast down".
........and, they "overcame" him, by.....
'THE BLOOD'... of 'JESUS THE CHRIST'...
and by the "word" of their 'Testimony'."

Revelation 12:10, 11.

"Except for... "THE PRESENCE OF THE LORD…"
….. nothing happens."